WHAT HURT DIDN'T HINDER

WHAT HURT DIDN'T HINDER

A Memoir

SHAN FOSTER

CONTENTS

Dedication:

To my village, who helped me overcome: my heartbeat and foundation, Gwendolyn and Manford Miller; those who sacrificed everything for me, Dr. Anita Foster-Horne, John and Stephanie Brown, my big-sisters-as aunts Tamara and Tracye. To my accountability partners, Micah and Dr. Sanica Matthews. To my fearless mentor, Sharon K. Roberson. To the reasons behind everything I do: Senimon, Jacoby, Amaria, Alexandria, Ashanti, and John Jr. — and my second chance at love, my wife Ariele.

Prologue

My dad gave me the Rudyard Kipling poem "If" at my high school graduation, just a few months before I headed off to Vanderbilt University. The poem is inspirational for a number of reasons, but my dad gave it to me at that point in my life because I was about to become a man. Not the man that the world would try to make me, but the man described in the poem — a man who can face defeat and get back up again, a man who can live his truth even when it's difficult. That day, it represented love and commitment.

I was seventeen, and like many young men of that age, the world was already trying to shape me into a certain kind of man based on what I did, especially when it came to my abilities as a basketball player. I hadn't played a single game as a Commodore, but people were already treating me like I was a star. Although I was headed to Vandy to play basketball, my dad understood that the sport was just a vehicle to take me through my four years of college and on to becoming the man I was destined to be.

When Dad gave me this poem, I wasn't sure what being a man truly meant in real life, much less the added intricacies of being a Black man. It wasn't until later in my life that I realized the depth of this poem and, more importantly, the complexity of its author, Kipling. My many years of traditional English classes never explained that this man, who wrote something so meaningful, could also promote white supremacy and racist ideology. Such dualities continue to define my life to this day.

Does being a man mean being physically strong? Not being too emotional? Attracting as many women as you can? Having courage? Commanding a crowd or being in charge? Making a good living?

When thinking about what it means to be a Black man, the questions are even more complicated. What happens if I get stopped by the police? Am I perceived to be a threat to others? Does my presence around a woman produce fear? Is my success so intimidating that it needs to be stopped?

While some of these "masculine" traits are healthy, others can be harmful to a man and everyone around him. What many people fail to realize is that a lot of this harm is done when our culture forces men and boys to choose between two extremes — he can do what a "man" does or else be seen as weak, and risk getting ridiculed or cast out by their peers.

There's the idea that there's no way to fall in the middle — you have to choose one or the other.

This all or none thinking can push boys to act out in unhealthy ways and push men to react based on past negative experiences. Men often abuse partners because they haven't been able to process their trauma; teenaged boys are pressured to have sex before they're ready, so they don't get made fun of; and very young boys might feel that the only way to get a bully off their back is to retaliate, sometimes violently.

If these men and boys look to others for answers, they might not find them. There aren't classes in how to handle the struggles of growing up, and society — whether it's through social media or politics or traditional media — only reinforces the "either-or" mindset that got them into a bad place from the start. Even if a man is presented with another option, he might see that alternative as a bridge too long to cross.

I've been caught between two extremes time and time again throughout my life, in environments ranging from a household experiencing domestic violence, to the NBA, to the corporate world. I've done things that I knew deep down weren't right, so I wouldn't be seen as "weak," and I've fallen to the pressure to be a certain way with women, which hurt and disrespected them deeply.

With the support of others, I was able to fight my way through these challenges to find healthy masculinity that creates better things in the world. I'm still a work in progress, but many men aren't as lucky. Men who never experienced the liberation of a healthy version of manhood perpetuate various forms of violence against women, and the young men who are exposed to those men are at risk of continuing the cycle of violence.

Now, my mission in life is to show men that there's no one way to be a man. You can be emotional or quiet or a pacifist, but that doesn't make you any less than other men. By opening up what "manhood" is and giving men the space to talk about things that we've stayed away from as a society, we can lift everyone up.

In telling my story, I hope you see that you aren't alone in what you're going through. You don't have to have the either-or mindset when it comes to your own masculinity or anything else in your life. I want to open your eyes to the possibilities that lie beyond our fears.

CHAPTER 1

My Foundation

My grandmother likes the old saying, *when life gives you lemons, make lemonade*, and in a lot of ways it sums up my early childhood.

I was born on August 20th, 1986 in Laurel, Mississippi to Anita Foster and John Brown, both college students. Since they weren't ready to be parents and needed to finish their education, my grandparents, Gwen and Manford Miller, took me in when I was nine months old. Sending me to live with my grandparents was possibly the most important decision that my parents could have made for me since they, my grandparents, gave me a stable beginning.

It was nearly impossible for my parents to balance being college students and raising a baby, though they tried. They even lived with me in student housing for a while. My grandmother had lived with her own parents after she and my mother's father split up and understood just how much of an impact that had made on her and her daughters' lives. Passing those blessings along was only natural.

Starting from when I was nine months old, I was at my grandmother's home in Slidell most of the time. Slidell, Louisiana is a small town about half an hour outside of New Orleans, with one main road that leads to everywhere you could possibly need to go. My grandmother and my grandfather had gotten married not long before I arrived, and thankfully he was more than happy to help her with the responsibilities of raising her grandchild. I was her first, and she wanted me to be close to her instead of with a babysitter.

My grandmother is the type of person that others gravitate towards and respect. Very few people stand up for what they believe in like she does. Once, the school where she taught didn't plan to celebrate Martin Luther King Jr. Day. "Well," my grandmother said, "if they aren't going to cancel classes for this, I just won't come in."

And she'll tell you the straight-up truth, even when you might not be ready to hear it. But she never says it to cause harm — she cares too much to let you go about your life without hearing an honest opinion. I was on the receiving end of that truth throughout my life, — I remember the time I went to play basketball overseas in Italy and brought my girlfriend with me. My grandmother wasn't a fan of "shacking up" because she felt like it led to sex before marriage and possibly even to having kids. We had some deep, difficult conversations about it, and while I didn't agree with her, I'm glad I can always depend on my grandmother to tell me how she truly feels.

She's dependable, all-around. If you need help with your kids, she'll be there. If you're sick and need a hot meal, she'll be there. And if you're at a crossroads (and can handle the truth), she'll reassure you that God has a plan for you. ·

My grandfather is the same way — he's kind and honest, but much more reserved. He'll talk and be cordial, of course, but he's a man of few words. Even when talking on the phone, he doesn't stay on very long. He keeps things simple and doesn't mince words.

He doesn't have to speak much, since his actions speak for him. He's all about doing what's right, even if it means going against the crowd. When I was growing up, he never laughed at jokes made at other people's expense, even if everyone else did. If my uncle, who had a car shop next door, started talking about women in a way that was inappropriate, my grandfather was quick to tell him, "that's not right."

His work ethic was second to none, too, and still is. He didn't just show up to his job as a bricklayer — he showed up early, his best foot forward, and made sure every single brick was lined up with careful precision. He applied that same care when building many of the houses our family friends and fellow churchgoers lived in. If you needed something fixed, or if you needed help in general, he'd show up with his tools. And as a deacon in the church, he was there to help people with the problems that a hammer couldn't fix.

Both together and individually, my grandparents were pillars of our town. They knew everyone, and everyone looked up to them. With their deep ties to others in our community, they established a village of supportive adults in my life.

The most important things that my grandparents wanted me to have were stability and discipline. Living with them meant that stability revolved around church. When I say we were in church literally all the time, I mean pretty much *all* the time. It didn't matter whether it was prayer service, choir rehearsal, Bible study, a deacon's meeting or Sunday school — my family was there.

The church where I grew up, Macedonia Baptist Church, could hold around 150 people and was often filled close to capacity every week. It was a place where I felt safe and loved — it was truly a family church. My grandfather helped to build the church and its baptismal pool, where I was baptized as a child. My grandmother and my aunts Tracye and Tamara were in the choir. My late great-uncle, the Reverend Dr. W.L. Russell, was the church's original founder. Missionary work was a huge part of our church as well. If there were opportunities to preach anywhere close to Mississippi or Louisiana, we'd go.

And it wasn't just that we went to church together, came home, and left it at that. Church was a part of the fabric of our life. After church, we'd sit down in the living room or the kitchen and talk about what we learned or what we did. Sitting there on the floor, surrounded by pictures of our family on the wall, we went beyond listening and discussed what it truly meant to be a Christian.

At that age, I wasn't a hundred percent sure of what I was listening to. I mean, I knew who Jesus was and I knew who God was. I could tell you a few stories from the Bible. I mostly just enjoyed the experience of it. I'd even go home and "play church" the way kids "play house." I would act like I was every person who spoke on the programs, from the deacons praying, to the announcements, to the choir.

This built my love of music too. I loved all the instruments the church had — the guitars, pianos, and drums. My family actually got me a guitar for Christmas, and a drum set too. I was a terrible player, but they knew I loved music, so they got them for me. I didn't take lessons; I just strummed whatever came to mind. I'm sure it didn't sound good at all. But everybody thought it was cute, so they let me strum my guitar so they could take pictures.

As I got older, the congregation let me play drums for the service from time to time, especially the song Amazing Grace. We played it every Sunday right before the reverend would preach, and I loved (and still love) that song. It didn't matter whether we were in Slidell or at our family church in Mississippi, Morning Start Baptist Church — it was some of the best music you'd ever hear. I would go home and reenact the songs.

Being so involved in church also gave me the perspective of people who openly worshipped and valued their relationship with God. Our church was a very expressive place, like many African-American churches are. When the spirit got high and people got excited, they'd dance or take a lap around the church. Some people even fell out so hard that they'd need help getting up. It wasn't about what you looked like to everyone else – it was just about connecting with God.

My peers shunned that kind of emotion – if you were doing that stuff, it was the topic of conversation for a long time, so I didn't show out the way the adults did. And if you looked crazy, they were going to crack jokes about you and any adults who got into it "too much." It wasn't cool to even talk about it. This was one of the first instances where I had to keep my authentic self hidden — there was a part of me that openly and willingly expressed myself in certain spaces, while another part of me shut down if there was a risk of being ridiculed. I had to keep quiet and hold some things in, even at that age. It was either that, or feel like an outsider.

Being in church so often meant that I became the church's kid too. To this day, members of the church ask my grandmother how I'm doing. Since I was usually one of only a few kids around (as my aunts were in high school and college), I spent time a lot of time surrounded by adults. I became extremely comfortable talking with older people and authority figures.

Looking back, being around adults really helped in my maturation, because I learned how important it is to speak my truth — no matter who I'm talking to. Spending so much time around adults, and grandparents in particular, helped me learn from their wisdom. They've lived long enough to have no fear of telling the truth. There's no regard for positions, titles, accolades, or status — they're just people — whether it was watching my grandmother tell the store manager that something wasn't priced correctly or hearing her talk to my school principal about how I was being treated by a teacher or other students. I've always been the person people called on to relay a message to an adult or authority figure, even today in the workplace.

But to be clear, I was still a child. My family loves to bring up an incident that happened when I was just turning five years old. There was a restaurant called Ryan's, an all-you-can-eat buffet, where kids could eat for free. We'd go out to dinner there as a family after church services or events. I had just turned five, but my family was set on me eating for free one more time because the age limit to eat for free was four years old.

The waitress asked, "How old are you?"

I knew the answer, since I'd had this conversation with my mom in the car. I said, "Well, I'm four when I'm at Ryan's, but I'm five when I'm at home."

Everyone thought it was the funniest thing...except for my mom, who laughed through her embarrassment. They ended up letting me eat for free one last time, but every time we went to Ryan's after that, the waiters reminded us of the time I'd been a little too honest.

There's another story my family likes to tell about a time when my age really showed – I was probably around four or five. My grandparents would often help to drive some of the more in-firmed elderly back to their homes after church services or events. There was a woman who had trouble getting in and out of vehicles, particularly ones that were low to the ground. Since I was already growing pretty tall for my age, I was asked to help people get in and out of cars. In this instance, I walked over to open the door for a woman to help her get into the car.

She waved me off and said, "No baby, it's okay. I appreciate it, but I don't need any help. I got it."

So I said, "Okay, cool," but with an attitude.

We got into the car and drove to where we were going. Before my grandparents could say anything, the woman asked, "Can you come over and help me get out of the car?"

I replied, "No, you got into this car by yourself, so you can get out of this car by yourself."

Everyone fell out laughing, but I ended up getting in trouble for being disrespectful. My grandparents were very fair when it came to discipline. They didn't try to intimidate me into doing better or make me feel terrible. They knew I would make mistakes, and took the time to explain exactly why I was being punished the way I was. In some ways, being acquainted with that kind of discipline made it harder to accept the harshness I would experience outside of the safe bubble they'd created.

While I learned a lot from the women in my family and community, my grandfather was one of the first people to teach me how to be a man. Having him around to help me was an enormous blessing on both a practical and emotional level, since my grandmother had mostly daughters. He helped out with things like potty training and being a gentleman.

He did everyday things like opening doors for people, or praying over every meal we had as a family. He'd bring back even the smallest flower for my grandmother just to make her smile. Even though he's not talkative, he's always clearly communicating how much he supports and loves all of us.

My grandfather wasn't afraid to get his hands dirty — literally. I remember his usual khakis, neatly pressed white shirt, work boots and hard hat being covered in clay or mud. Even in the scorching Louisiana heat, he worked all day, starting at five a.m. On the days he'd take me to work with him, I'd watch him cut bricks and place each one in the right spot, constantly measuring and checking to ensure that everything was perfect.

On one of those days where I watched him work, he told me, "This is what hard work looks like. It's not easy, and yes, it takes a little sweat. But if you work at it, you can be good at it and make good money to support your family."

This lesson was particularly important for me growing up, since it carried over into many areas of my life, from my athletic career to my work advocating against domestic violence. To this day, I believe if I work hard, I can succeed at anything.

Though my grandfather was there day-to-day, I don't want to discount the way my father positively shaped my view of what it means to be a man in these early days. Although he and my mother split up, he never tried to get out of his responsibilities as a father and always came through on his promises. On Fridays he'd take me to spend time with him where he lived in Gulfport, Mississippi and take me home on Sundays, sometimes taking me to see his mom and other family members. I always packed the night before and occasionally would go to sleep wearing the clothes I wanted to wear the next day, just so we could leave faster. I'd check the window frequently, especially if I heard a car coming down the road.

Like for my grandparents, church was a very important part of my father's life, which meant it was always a part of my life, no matter where I was. In our long talks, he'd reinforce the Christian mindset that I'd gotten from my grandparents, reminding me to respect my authority figures, turn the other cheek, and treat every single person with respect and kindness.

My father and I would play games on the Super Nintendo all night, and it took years for me to finally beat him. Video games are yet another outlet that kept me out of trouble, since it's harder to get into bad situations when you're sitting in front of a screen. I'm still big into video games today, and I credit them for sparking my competitive spirit.

One of the biggest connections my father and I had came from our love of sports — football, baseball, boxing, and of course, basketball. He had played basketball in both high school (where he finished as the #2 player in all of Mississippi) and in college at University of Southern Mississippi. Whenever I was with him, he only fed my love of basketball, a love that had started in Slidell with my grandparents.

When my family wasn't at church, we were watching Michael Jordan's Chicago Bulls. This was in the era when they were winning championships left and right. I'd go outside and try to do the same things he and his teammates did using a hole I'd made in one of my grandmother's bushes. She didn't appreciate that, so she had my grandfather put up a backboard and rim on the chimney on the side of the house where there was enough pavement for me to play.

As I got better, the ball would sometimes hit the window of the house, so eventually, he moved the backboard to a tree trunk. My grandfather wasn't a big basketball player, but he took great joy in the happiness the game brought me, smiling and cracking jokes that my moves looked just like Michael Jordan's.

My aunt Tamara (who we call Marsha) was my first "coach." Since we weren't too far apart in age, she was more like my sister than my aunt. She wasn't a big basketball player either and didn't play in school, but she knew the fundamentals – dribbling with both hands, shooting jump shots and free throws, using the backboard, things like that.

We'd play one-on-one or HORSE, and she'd win every time. She'd talk trash after beating me, but every now and again, she'd give me advice like, "Hit the top of the square and it will go in every time" or "Stay out here and practice until you make 5 in a row. Then shoot your free throws. You gotta be able to make those. They're free!" I couldn't wait until I was good enough to beat her, so I practiced and practiced.

Dad helped bring that practice into focus. The advice he gave laid the foundation of my game, even though it would be years until I started coming into my full potential. He didn't just teach me the basics. He taught me strategies, like seeing the floor, thinking a play ahead, and reading situations, plus some softer skills like the value of sportsmanship and losing with grace.

He always had me thinking of what was next by showing me the importance of setting goals. For basketball, it was getting more playing time and scoring. For my grades, it was doing better and better throughout the year. Later on, his insights about setting goals and figuring out what I truly wanted would help me through some of the most important decisions I've ever made.

When my father got married and had kids with my stepmother Stephanie, he wanted me to get to know my other siblings, Amaria, Alexandria, Ashanti, and John Jr. when they came along. Now I was big brother to others along with my siblings Senimon and Jacoby on my mother's side. Having spent the first six years of my life as an only child, I was more than ready for the consistent entertainment my siblings could bring.

I played outside with Senimon and Jacoby, taking our dog Precious along to watch us play football. When we got back in, we'd play on our bunk beds, pushing Jacoby onto the bottom bunk and goofing around. I visited my other siblings in Mississippi every summer like clockwork, though for a long time it was just Amaria, the oldest. We got to do special things that they didn't do much when I wasn't there, like going out to eat as a family, going to the beach, or staying up late playing video games. For my siblings who lived with my dad, it was like a vacation from the norm.

Those moments were precious to me, especially since I only got to see my siblings on my dad's side each summer. As I grew up, they became my inspiration to do better. I knew that they looked up to me just because I was their older brother, so I did my best to be the role model that they needed, especially when it came to achieving dreams that seemed impossible.

In general, the adults in my life stressed how important loving your family was. If you grow up loving your siblings and cousins, then you know how to love other people. If you can't love your family, then loving others is that much harder. My grandparents made sure to bring me around my extended family often, taking me to Mississippi to stay for a while during the holidays or birthdays. Everyone in my family is hilarious – they'll tease you, but it's always too funny for you to get mad about it. Family gatherings and conversations running from lighthearted to serious advice are what make me feel alive, even to this day.

My grandparents created the kind of environment where I could understand what healthy masculinity really meant. I was always around women who were authority figures, showing me that respect for women was non-negotiable. The men in my life only exemplified that respect, consistently. The conversations men had were still "masculine" – sports and work were common topics, as was joking around – but they weren't centered around negativity or talking about women in disrespectful ways or how strong they were. They were all about their families and their communities. They supported one another and worked hard, giving to their community to raise everyone up.

I wasn't exposed to the pressures that make many men feel as if they have to make destructive choices. I didn't have to choose between two bad options – being a man in a way that didn't feel right to me or being shut out -- like I would in the years to come. It wasn't all about being in control all the time, or being the toughest one out there or holding in your emotions to save face (with a few exceptions). It was about being yourself and making those around you feel loved and supported.

Knowing what I do now about people, it was a unique experience and I was probably sheltered from the toxic things that took place. People were generally on their best behavior around me, especially since I had a smart mouth as a child and would repeat things that I thought would get a laugh around people. Plus, church came with a lot of expectations surrounding how people should behave. Acting outside of that led to quick consequences, which no one wanted.

My grandparents' home was a place where I was protected and could learn from my mistakes. Even though I only spent my first six years living with them, I learned many of the things that I still hold true today about faith, integrity, education, athleticism, and work ethic. It's where I got my sense of humor. It's where I learned that so many others sacrifice and give to allow me to fulfill my dreams. It was where I learned how to love.

But when I turned six years old, my mother came home with a man she had married, Michael, and told me we were going to live together as a family in Jackson, Mississippi. I didn't go to the wedding and neither did my grandparents. I loved my mom, but I'd come to love living with my grandparents too. Leaving felt like turning my back on everyone and everything that was Shan.

But I was just six years old – I didn't have any choice in the matter. I had to accept it, even though part of me already knew that things would never be the same.

CHAPTER 2

The Storm

I wanted to go back to my grandparents' house the minute I arrived in Jackson.

Looking at it from an adult's perspective, it made sense for me to make the move when I did. I had just finished kindergarten, and it wouldn't have made sense for me to bounce around from school to school. But as a kid, nothing added up. I already felt like I had two dads — my grandfather and my biological father. And now I had to call this stranger "dad"? This stranger who was the reason why I'd been uprooted from what felt like home? That felt off to me, even as a young kid.

Michael was what some may call a very traditional "manly man" — he epitomized gender stereotypes. He was a big, athletic guy with these huge biceps and forearms. He would often talk about the things that he had to do as a child, like pulling tractors, hunting, tending to livestock and all kinds of crazy stuff, and all the physical feats he was capable of. I never saw him do any of those things, so who knew if he was telling the truth or just trying to make himself look more macho.

He didn't start out all that bad — he bought nice gifts for Christmas and birthdays, and eventually he and my mom had my younger siblings, Senimon and Jacoby. He introduced me to organized sports through the neighborhood recreation center and even tried to teach me some sports moves he learned growing up. Unfortunately, the teaching methods he used (and many of the other things he did) were more like a form of coercive control. He was a guy who exerted his will over every situation, using both his size and his demeanor.

His voice made you feel small, no matter how loud or soft it was. When he yelled, you knew he was trying to push you back into what he thought was your place — beneath him. But, his "calm" voice was worse — that was just the quiet before the real storm hit.

It was incredibly important that he was in control; whatever he said was what happened. It didn't matter what the situation was or who it involved. He had to be "the man." For Michael, giving up control, even if that was the reasonable thing to do, meant being weak. He always needed everything to go his way, just to feed his ego and put up whatever front he wanted people to see.

He'd invite our neighbors over for a barbecue, going all out with ribs and pulled pork, making sure our guests were comfortable and had everything they needed — the perfect host. Those were great days. But the next day, it was right back to yelling and putting his own need for control over everyone else's comfort. My mother would leave, but then she would come back.

At one point, when Momma had just left him for the first of two times, Michael joined our church and became an usher. For at least two weeks everyone saw his smiling face when they came in to worship, but once Mom came back, he stopped going. Nothing he did was ever as it seemed.

My dad has always been a part of my life, and he didn't want my mother getting married to change that. But Michael immediately put new rules in place, namely that instead of talking directly to Momma about me, my dad would have to talk to him. The other new rule was that he didn't want my dad coming to pick me up on a regular basis, the way he did when I lived with my grandparents in Slidell.

Eventually, Dad married my stepmother Stephanie and started a family with her, so he tolerated the first rule, but he still wasn't as accepting of Michael's second rule. Dad wanted what was best for my mom's relationship because by extension, that would affect me; at the same time, he needed to talk and see me on a regular basis.

Michael claimed that if he controlled when I could speak to my dad, it would let me get closer to his side of the family. As an adult I now know that Michael, as with most abusers, was attempting to isolate us from my dad to have total control over the family.

If my father wasn't the honest, straightforward man he is, I might have gone on believing Michael's lies. Dad didn't try to hide the truth from me — he tried to convince Michael there was plenty of my time to go around. Michael had me every single day, my dad said, and could shape me in ways that he himself wouldn't be able to. The least Michael could do, my dad told him, would be to let us speak one-on-one.

Eventually Michael did let us connect, but still, Dad didn't come around as often as he had when I was in Slidell. He knew I was smart enough to figure out that Michael was the reason he kept his distance. It certainly wasn't because he didn't want to see me.

Even as a kid, I could tell Michael was jealous of my dad. Dad was, and still is, a great man. He was the valedictorian of his high school class, played basketball in college, and lived a Godly life. He exemplified the values that my grandparents had instilled in me in the early years of my life — respect, integrity, and a strong work ethic.

Dad's positive influence was a threat to Michael's power and control. He took every opportunity to remind me of the things he did for me, just to show how much we all needed him. When he opened gifts from us on his birthday or Father's Day, he would say thank you and add, "All I try to do is keep a roof over y'all's head and make sure you never have to want for anything." Or he'd explain everyone's role in the house, saying, "My job is to keep the lights on, your job is to do good in school, get your chores done, and look after your brother and sister."

To be clear, everything he did or said wasn't bad or detrimental. Just like no one is perfect, no one is *all* bad. However, the complexities of manhood are just as diverse as the world. They're a combination of various ideals, principles, values, actions and behaviors, most of which aren't fully understood by the majority of men. Yet, the lack of balance can have a disproportionate effect on the cognitive development of children. Unfortunately for me, this new example of manhood was unbalanced, weighted heavily in the opposite direction from the examples in my younger years.

Michael didn't have time for tears. "You want to cry? Go talk to your Momma. Come back and talk to me when you can be a man about it" or, "I can't handle no son who's going to be a pussy" were his responses to any emotional expression.

So I had to "man up." There wasn't space to be anything but "a man." I either handled it — even though I didn't know how — or I'd get verbally abused. Both options were terrible.

Everything seemed to be an opportunity for Michael to show he was in control by making someone else out to be in trouble. Usually, it was me. It didn't matter whether I was talking back, talking too much at school — the consequence was often a whooping. I wasn't even a bad kid. I looked around the neighborhood I lived in and there were kids who were being suspended or expelled, kids who were picked up by the police for fighting, or worse. I did none of those things, yet I was beaten regularly and severely.

I didn't understand it. It was so drastically different than what I experienced in my grandparents' home. While they didn't shy away from disciplining me, they would usually talk it through to help me understand why things were wrong, why I shouldn't do whatever I had done, or how I should respect women and elders. I didn't understand how this man, who was not my biological father, or my grandparents or my mother, had the authority to torture me in this way.

I had no choice but to endure. That's just the way it was, even though I didn't like it. I didn't have any power or authority.

As time went on, I witnessed a lot of arguing, yelling, and screaming. I don't remember what most of the arguments were about, but they were a constant in the background of my life. Their main dynamic was around Michael asking Momma to do things. If she didn't do as he asked, there was an argument, and even if she did — whether it was cooking or cleaning or something else, he only responded with a "that's what you're supposed to do, woman!"

I don't remember ever seeing them cuddle while watching a movie or expressing anything that seemed like affection in their day-to-day interactions. That isn't to say it never happened, but I can't think of a time where I saw it.

The only good moments I can remember were at the barbecues on the weekend. He wasn't just a good host at those times, he was genuinely great on the grill and at cooking breakfast, and he took great pride in those skills. Aside from those times, everything revolved around him being the king of the house — he set the tone and everyone else had to play their role. Watching TV, we all had to sit quietly and be perfectly still as he smoked through his daily pack of cigarettes and drank his favorite beer, Heineken. If anything was out of line, he'd say something right away and expected it to be fixed immediately.

We were all bound to whatever Michael decided. Whatever he wanted to do is what happened. Eventually we moved from Mississippi to Metairie, Louisiana, right outside of New Orleans. The move didn't make things any better.

I really wanted to run away. Since Senimon and Jacoby were younger than me and I didn't have many close friends my age, my only confidant was a hundred-and-twenty pound Rottweiler named Precious. She became my best friend and my outlet. I would sit and cuddle with her, telling her everything I thought — how I wanted to go back to Slidell, how things would be much better if I did, or how things would be if I lived with my dad.

Once I actually attempted to run away. I had no plan. I was going to try to get to my grandparents' house, but I didn't know how. I didn't have a vehicle or any other form of transportation. I was tired of having to sit on my hands at school because my butt was still sore from being beaten so badly the day before. I was tired of needing to stay out of the house just to try to stay sane. I was tired of hurting.

I gathered up the courage to finally leave, talking to some of my friends about it before I made the attempt. One of them was Jose, who lived across the street from us and would often play basketball with me and the other kids in the neighborhood. That day, Michael came home early and noticed I wasn't there — I was hiding in Jose's backyard with all my bags. He stormed outside, trying to track me down. "Has anybody seen Shan?" Michael asked my friends when he couldn't find me.

"Yeah, he's in my backyard," Jose said.

I think Jose really had my best interest at heart — he knew I wasn't the type of kid who would survive being on the streets on my own. But still, he'd unwittingly set me up for one of the most miserable nights of my life.

I came out of Jose's backyard with my stuff, so it was obvious that I was trying to go somewhere. I walked back to my house, and the minute I reached the top of the front steps, Michael slapped me on the back of my head and made me fall inside.

"Go into your room, take off your clothes and get ready for this whooping," he said in that deceptively calm voice.

I had no choice. I was powerless. I went into the room, already crying because I knew it was going to be bad. I took off all my clothes and knelt down next to the bed. He came in with some yellow rope, then tied up my hands and ankles with it. Then he beat me with his belt for what seemed like hours. I'm sure it was much less time than that, but it felt like it would never end. I yelled and screamed so much that the neighbors' dogs barked and tried to jump over the fence to come save me.

But of course, they couldn't. I had to lay there and take it. Eventually, he finished.

"Don't you ever try to leave this house again. And if you tell anybody, it'll be worse," he said. And then, he added, "I only do this because I love you."

This was far from love. The love I had known from my grandparents was safe and filled with respect and kindness. Michael's "love" was control and dominance. Love did not look or feel like a bruised and battered body.

To this day, I don't know why I was treated the way I was. Jacoby and Senimon weren't treated nearly as badly as I was. Maybe because they were his biological children and I wasn't. Maybe it has something to do with the way he was treated as a child, but I don't know for sure. Now I've learned that hurt people hurt others and the non-biological child of an abuser is often targeted.

This behavior is not right and is actually illegal. However, what is a child to do when the cultural norm is "what happens in our house stays in our house," and excuses are made by adults when signs of abuse are normalized? It's heartbreaking to hear stories of colleagues who endure child abuse, rape, sexual molestation, and other forms of abuse by members of their families. What's worse is that until now, we've all shared the same response of never talking about what happened. I've learned that whether we talk about it or not, the effects of this lived trauma are very real and that it impacts our lives, relationships, and behaviors until we make healing and forgiveness a priority.

Michael tried to hide his abuse from my mother. I don't know if she knew. I believe she should have known. Perhaps she didn't see the abuse he inflicted on me. I want to believe she didn't know until later, as I shared my experience.

The only good memories of those years were outside of that house or when I visited my grandparents. I couldn't wait to go to school, just so I didn't have to deal with being targeted. I got involved in every possible activity I could at church, from the choir to the youth department. Anything they asked me to do, I did because anything was better than being at home. No one ever knew my real motivation for always showing up.

Basketball became way more than something I liked to watch and play — it was my way to stay out of the house as much as possible. I was in middle school, and it was the first time I was playing organized basketball on a team. I was growing at a rapid pace, probably due to DNA from my dad — he was 6'8" and played basketball, so I attribute some of my athleticism to him.

I made the team and though I wasn't very good at that point, I took every opportunity to play on a team, to go to every practice and to do extra workouts. Basketball was a passion, and it gave me the chance to let out my negative frustrations from home in a positive way.

My passion for basketball also had a positive effect on my grades. My mom was very serious about education and made it clear that in order for me to play, I had to keep up my grades. Once I brought home a C on my report card and she didn't let me play in a tournament, despite my coach's pleading.

Life outside the house had its own set of difficulties, particularly when it came to fitting in. I saw that my peers subscribed to the same ideas of manhood and masculinity as Michael did, a way of life that was very black and white with no way to sit anywhere in between.

Just as I'd felt a split between the person I was at church in Slidell and the person I was with my peers, I now felt like I had to be a different person depending on the situation I was in.

Our neighborhood was rough, and back then New Orleans had one of the highest murder rates in the United States. Surviving there, especially with kids who could be harsh, meant that my manhood was going to be challenged every single day.

Always, the question was are you a man or not? If you're a man, you'll stand up for yourself. You'll fight if you need to. You'll exert your will in such a way that others are scared to mess with you. The most socially acceptable way of dealing with conflict was to fight, because backing down or walking away meant being bullied.

Kids can be cruel everywhere, but especially in New Orleans. They made fun of my clothes, my shoes, my big ears and feet, my haircut, my book bag, the way I walked, the relationship I had with teachers, and my family. They even made up a song about me because my pants stopped higher than my ankles since my parents couldn't really afford to buy clothes often enough to keep up with my growth spurts. "Nickels, nickels, quarters, quarters, Shan got on high waters." Nothing was off limits.

On top of the teasing, I felt stuck between two environments without fitting fully into either one — the basketball team and the honors classes. The kids on the basketball team were less academically focused, usually joking around or choosing to shoot hoops instead of studying. The kids in my honors classes were the total opposite. I was too nerdy for the basketball team, but too cool for my honors classes. Standing out in that way put a target on my back that other kids tried to hit — by calling me names and generally making my life difficult. I had a choice: I could just sit there and take it, or I could be a "man." I could be in trouble either with my peers or at home.

I was already being punished at home most of the time so I figured, "Hey, it is what it is." There was a period where I got a negative behavior report every single day. These reports were supposed to be signed by our parents, but I kept them in a big stack in my room under my bed and made excuses as to why I never brought them back. Eventually the school called, and my mom asked me to show her the reports I'd been hiding.

I wasn't a bad kid — I was a kid trying to fit in and trying to survive. I wanted to do what was right, but a lot of times, doing what was right only made me an outcast. It's a tough choice at that age. I didn't want to be the kid who didn't have any friends. I wanted to be in the In Crowd and I wanted people to like me. Most kids want to fit in, and they often struggle with this feeling until they find a group where they feel a sense of belonging.

I felt isolated and alone, even though I'm sure other kids felt the same way to a certain degree. My siblings were too young to understand, and my mom was in survival mode because of her relationship and the challenges of raising three children. I had no one to turn to.

I juggled these masks outside of my home life, while inside things continued to deteriorate. By the time I was a freshman in high school, Momma was beginning to see that she no longer wanted to be in that relationship. I'll never forget the turning point for her.

One night she and Michael were fighting as they usually did. I never saw him physically put his hands on her, but judging by the way he treated me and the aggressive, controlling tone he used with her, I assume he did so behind closed doors. In my work to end violence against women, I've learned that abuse isn't just physical — it also involves the intimidation, name-calling, and control that we were all put through constantly.

Momma decided that she was going to take me and my siblings to my grandmother's house. The three of us were sitting on the couch, all packed up and ready to go, when Michael decided that he wasn't going to let us go anywhere. He grabbed my mom, but she got away. In a second attempt to get away, she took her keys and threw them in his face, putting a gash in his forehead. Momma then called the police, which meant we had to stay and wait for them to show up.

At that time, if the police came to a house due to domestic violence, somebody had to go to jail. The policy was created to add a level of accountability to officers who tended to give verbal warnings instead of taking action against perpetrators. A verbal warning meant no police report would be filed and nothing would really be done, which discouraged victims from reporting in the first place. If police made an arrest, however, a police report had to be filed.

That day, the person who was arrested was my mother.

I'll never forget seeing her in handcuffs, tears running down her face. "You're going to let them take me to jail in front of my kids?"

As bad as things were, I knew they were about to get much worse. I was scared, but knew I had to be there for Jacoby and Senimon since they were too young to understand. I told them everything was going to be alright, that we just had to pray for God to bring Mom back home safe, and that I was there to protect them no matter what. At the same time, I wanted to be honest with them; I wanted to tell them what a horrible person their father was and about all of the suffering he'd caused.

At that time, my only concept of jail was that it was a very bad place where people didn't come back. I felt sick with fear whenever I thought of what might happen to her. All I could do was watch her get put into the police car and see them drive away.

I missed my mom terribly. I had to stay home that night in the same place all of these horrible things had happened — I wasn't allowed to sleep at other people's homes, ever. I didn't want to think about what life would be like with just him, the monster I had no desire to spend even a second around.

I also knew I couldn't leave because Senimon and Jacoby needed me more than ever. Since our mom and Michael worked a lot, we were always close. As the oldest, I was the one they came to when they were going through something, but they felt protective of me in some ways too. Since so much of our environment was chaotic, both in the house and outside, we could always depend on each other, even if we fought.

I had a basketball game the day after my mom was arrested and it was by far the worst game I've ever played in my life. I didn't score a single point the first half. I was dropping passes and missing shots that I would usually make. I was just completely out of it.

But at halftime, she came. I'll never forget that. She was dressed in black jeans and a black leather coat. I spotted her through the locker room window and ran to give her a huge hug. She told me everything was going to be okay, and even though she didn't stay for the rest of the game, I had a much better second half.

And thankfully, this incident was the final straw. I helped her pack and we left to get a fresh start.

I have mixed feelings about the experiences I've had; they were hard, but they made me resilient. I learned that very few things were going to be as bad as my childhood, so if I could get through that, I could get through anything. It took me a long time to forgive Michael. I do forgive him, but I have not forgotten. It took a long time for me to forgive my mom, and even now I don't blame her completely.

Many times, we underestimate the effect that trauma has on us and how we show up everyday. If you're not aware of those effects, then you're probably not aware of how they're affecting other people. But what you go through doesn't have to define you. What you go through can be the adversity that's necessary to fuel your passion and give you the discipline to be great.

I have no doubt that the struggles I went through helped me to be a professional basketball player. If things hadn't been so rough at home, I wouldn't have spent so much time playing and practicing long after everyone else went home.

The foundation of my faith helped me endure as well. I spent a lot of time in prayer and a lot of time talking to my dog Precious, just getting it out. Letting all of my feelings out instead of just handling it "like a man" made a huge difference in how I felt. It doesn't have to be told to another person, but letting everything out can be liberating.

The way men are raised to not talk about their feelings and to shoulder things on their own can cause more problems than people talk about. Since emotions like fear or loneliness don't line up with traditional views of manliness, men sometimes turn that anger on themselves or onto others. And even if men do see that their emotions are the problem, many don't see the point in talking about them — they may even believe that talking about problems will make them seem bigger. [1]

If men aren't allowed to process their feelings, they won't know how to ask for what they really need in their relationships or careers. Men might benefit from talking to someone when they have a problem, but how will they know it'll help if they don't feel like they can try it? On the more extreme end, if men don't know how to handle anger or rejection, they could end up lashing out violently on the people closest to them, usually a spouse, child, or people they manage at work.

For me, having examples of healthy masculinity and maintaining my faith in my life helped put the negative experiences into perspective. I saw that there was another path outside of the two extremes, which over time allowed me to define masculinity for myself. If I hadn't had those positive role models early on, I would have given up, and the next few years of my life might not have played out the way they did.

Our family was moving out of a fire, but the embers were still there.

CHAPTER 3

Moving On

My mom leaving Michael right around the time I became a teenager represented a new chapter for all of us, one I was eager to enter. What I didn't know was that this healing process would take some time and leave lingering effects.

In our new life, Mom had to be everything for everyone — a mother, a father, a student, and an employee — without a break. I had additional responsibilities too. I babysat a lot while Mom was in class or at work, cooking simple things like macaroni and cheese or fried pork chops for Senimon and Jacoby.

My grandmother says I've always been a protector, even from a young age, and these new circumstances gave me the opportunity to fully step into that role. I looked back at how my grandfather was a leader in his house. He was always there, setting a tone of respect, hard work, love and consistency. I knew I had to do the same.

I couldn't just be gone all the time as an escape anymore. I had to be a positive role model for my siblings. Since Senimon was older now, I helped her understand why her parents weren't together and why she needed to take school seriously. She took the split the hardest, and I knew she needed someone to lean on. Our bond got so solid that today we call each other when something difficult happens, sometimes even before we know anything is wrong.

I taught Jacoby how to play video games because I'd noticed how much they helped me stay out of trouble. Gaming also helped me to learn competitiveness, focus, and quick decision-making, which I wanted to pass along to him. These moments brought us closer together and we still love to play together today.

At the same time, there was a disconnect between my mom and me. I loved her so much, but I saw that she'd become a different person, perhaps as a result of her abusive relationship. Before her marriage to Michael, the time I spent with my mother was filled with joy and laughter. She was just like my grandmother. Afterwards, she became much more demanding and mean. She yelled and screamed at me for coming into the house after the streetlights came on, or for getting behavior reports for talking too much in school, or for not doing chores. It was as if she was trying to be her version of "tough" since there wasn't a man in the house anymore to play that role. I resented her for it. I was confused and hurt.

It was like she was in survival mode, and even though Michael was gone, there was a different pressure. Momma had to play the role of both parents and was solely responsible for everything.

She worked and went to school, believing that finishing college would mean a better life for all of us; she refused to quit (and eventually went on to earn her PhD). She got help from her friend Iris and others, and if we had to be at home while she was at work, Momma called us every hour to make sure we were okay.

On top of the environment of fear that Michael created, I was terrified that Momma could suddenly die or go unconscious. My mother's health had taken a bad turn during her relationship with Michael. Sometimes she would pass out for no clear reason, and Michael would have to put a cold towel on her head and neck to bring her back. She was young. Surely she wasn't going to die. All I could do was reassure Jacoby and Senimon that things would be okay, even though I wasn't sure of it myself.

Thankfully, it never happened again after she left him. Physical manifestations of psychological trauma aren't unheard of when it comes to victims of domestic violence. Survivors can sometimes experience a range of long-term health issues, from musculoskeletal problems, to neurological damage.[2] Women who report domestic violence are sometimes twice as likely as women who weren't abused to have chronic health conditions like respiratory disease, diabetes, and insomnia.[3] Knowing this makes me feel like there was a connection between her fainting episodes and the stress from her marriage.

None of this is to say that Momma didn't care. She made so many sacrifices to give us what we needed, sometimes going without food so we could eat. One of the biggest ways she supported me was to let me focus on basketball, even though I could have gotten a job to help support the family when I was old enough. Momma always made sure that I had all of the gear I needed and came to my games when she could. Even though I wasn't very good at the time, she saw my passion and wanted to support me.

I appreciate her so much for doing that. Had I been forced to work like many of my other friends and peers, I probably wouldn't have been the basketball player that I became. But at home, there was a disconnect between what was supportive sacrifice and how she treated me. She was short-tempered, often yelling about what I didn't do and not offering much praise for what I did well. It was like she was trying to inject toughness to make up for the fact that my dad couldn't be around all the time; in some ways, she was trying to make me "a man" and keep me safe.

More women find themselves in this situation than we care to admit. For single mothers, raising young men can be challenging, especially when society can be vicious in their dealings with them. In marginalized communities, the treatment of young men brings about an extra layer of trauma, concern, and fear. We're now aware of "the talk" that parents have with young men of color, in fear of their child losing his life to police brutality. Whether it's George Floyd, Jacob Blake, Ahmaud Arbery, or countless others, parents of children of color live in constant fear every time their child leaves the home. That fear produces heightened levels of anxiety, stress, and worry.

I knew my mother loved me, but her treatment of me was a far cry from what I'd experienced at my grandparents' house. My time with them shaped what love is and isn't to me, and taught me how to care for people. I hadn't experienced that in a long time. Eventually, I felt so overwhelmed and confused that I wrote

Momma a long letter. It basically said, "If you love me, why are you treating me this way?"

From her perspective, Momma always gave us space to talk to her face to face. However, she often didn't consider whether she was a welcoming person to talk to — at this time, she wasn't very approachable. But I needed answers, especially since I felt so stuck after my failed attempt at running away. A letter felt like the safest way to do that, and all I could do was hope she'd be receptive. It felt like my last chance. If the letter didn't go well, I planned to go live with my dad, even though it would be painful to be away from everyone. I just needed relief. This pain was too much of a burden for me, a child, or anyone else to shoulder.

I was so lost. I loved her, but I hated how she was acting. I now understand that it was because of the trauma she was experiencing, but I didn't then. I was a good kid — I taught myself piano, was on the honor roll and always active in church leadership. My classmates always voted me most likely to succeed. In my eyes, while I wasn't perfect, I was doing the right things, a lot.

In my letter, I detailed all the good things I did, listed the positive qualities that other adults said I had, and wrote about my plans to go to college. Then I gave it to her. I was willing to endure a lot to protect my siblings, but I still needed to know Momma loved me in order for me to stay.

Often, men and boys are asked to be the stoic ones and to not care about feelings like that, but that doesn't mean that the very human need to be loved and cared for goes away. I had been pushed to my limit and I couldn't shoulder that pain anymore.

I finally brought up the letter on a long drive to my grandparents' house when it was just the two of us. I remember the feelings more than the details of the conversation: my nervousness about how she received it, the tears we both shed as we opened up, the pain in Momma's voice when she told me about the weight on her shoulders raising me and my siblings alone, and having to make sacrifices every single day. And after she apologized for making me feel like she didn't love me, I remember feeling a new love and appreciation for her work ethic and strength. It felt like she needed the conversation as much as I did. I'm not sure of the impact it had on her, but for me, it changed everything. That one conversation made our relationship flourish, which made life as a family even better. Senimon still calls it "the time we were all together."

Soon, our new normal fell into place — my mother worked and provided, while I helped with my brother and sister and stayed out of trouble. We were a team with a game plan. I had basketball to give me some normalcy in the neighborhood and at school, and friends to help out when we needed it. I had priorities now. A Plan. Structure without chaos was the new normal.

I'm glad I took that leap and addressed my pain, because I'm not sure where we would be otherwise. It created a positive change in my other relationships too. I became someone who other people could lean on and talk to.

As a family, we had been through a textbook case of domestic violence. Now we had to move forward and start the true healing process.

As I got older, I mostly talked openly with my female friends, who were more willing to open up. Some I dated, some were just friends, and many called me their big brother. I didn't have to be hard with them — I could just be myself.

One of those friends was Sanica, who's one of my best friends to this day. We're both type-A personalities, so we can butt heads, but we've always been able to be open with each other. She'll tell me the truth whether I like it or not, and has always been another person I can lean on for support about anything. She also gives me a woman's view on things, which helps me notice where my male privilege might lead me astray.

Talking with my female friends has given me a perspective on how certain kinds of trauma can affect women. I had friends who experienced rape, teenage pregnancy, thoughts of suicide, and guilt about sex — areas I had no experience with. Helping in any way I could taught me how powerful a supportive relationship can be in changing someone's future.

My male friends were very different from my female friends. They were much more reluctant to talk about anything that was bothering them, so I learned to drop seeds and let someone else water them. I'd tell them my truth or how I felt about their situation and then quickly change the subject to sports, neighborhood drama, or some dispute between peers. At a later date I'd see that they used my advice. They'd never tell me themselves, but just knowing I helped made it worth it to me.

In my community, like many others, we didn't really talk about abusive relationships or other forms of trauma. We just moved on, scars and all, even if the situations put lives at stake.

I remember sitting at the window of our blue house with Jacoby and Senimon, and seeing a man get shot in the head after a drug deal went wrong. It shook us up, but we didn't fear playing outside the next day without an adult. There were other shootouts outside, times where we just had to huddle together because we were all we had. We made sure we were fine in the moment, but we didn't process the aftermath.

Outside of the most practical concerns, there was no going to counseling or sitting down as a family to talk about what things meant and how they were going to be. Most of us who experience this kind of trauma don't reflect on how the situation changes our emotional state. This lack of openness does a massive disservice for everyone involved — you can't patch up a wound in the dark.

When I talked to Senimon about our childhood when writing this book, she said she wished there had been someone there to help us process things so she didn't have to put on such a tough armor later in life. Without addressing the problem, you end up protecting yourself in ways that might not be the healthiest for you in the long run.

Violence is a widespread issue. Without exception, every race, ethnicity, socio-economic status and age group is affected by it. More than one in four women and more than one in ten men have experienced physical or sexual violence from a partner, and nearly half of all women and men in the United States have experienced psychological aggression by an intimate partner in their lifetime. [4]

In 60 to 75% of cases where a parent is physically abused, the children are abused as well.[5] Being exposed to such physical or psychological violence at such a young age can have serious negative implications for a child's mental and emotional development, leading to depression, anxiety, personality disorders, and poor academic outcomes. They're also much more likely to be affected by violence as adults, as either the victim or the perpetrator.[6]

And yet, we don't talk about it. For those who have left, the shame and guilt can be so overwhelming that they don't want to open up about it. Fear, isolation, intimidation, and threats of violence silence those who are still in those relationships. As I experienced growing up, opening up and talking about your feelings as a man was seen as weird or simply "not what a man does" — a view which might also prevent men from speaking up.

It's another either-or trap that men find themselves in time and time again. We're put to the test, often ending up in situations like the ones I found myself in, things I never spoke about until I wrote this book. If a man admits feelings like this, he likely won't receive the help he needs, or he'll get negative pushback. That snowballs, leading men to make decisions that negatively impact others or themselves because they don't know how, or feel that they can't, process their emotions. Without openly facing the reality of what domestic violence does to victims and their families, people can't heal and might continue the cycle.

Positive intervention from role models or healthy outlets can be the key that we need to end most forms of violence, including domestic and sexual violence. I found many of those role models through one of my life's greatest passions, basketball. I certainly needed them — high school tested me in ways I'd never expected.

CHAPTER 4

Wearing the Mask

Maintaining a number of personas was a necessity for me, and most kids, growing up in the outskirts of New Orleans. There was a different "me" for everyone, an idea explored in the 2015 documentary, *The Mask That You Live In*. "The mask" is the persona you put on to blend in, whether that persona reflects the real you or not.

I was one person when I was with my family or at church. I was fun to be around, loving on everyone around me and enjoying their conversation and stories. I cracked jokes about what was happening at church or something from a Bible story. We only listened to gospel music and loved watching The Cosby Show.

I was a completely different person when I was traveling the country playing basketball. I was more cocky, aggressive, and competitive — the typical "man's man." I talked about sports, girls, and material things with my friends, usually listening to rap by Lil Wayne, Juvenile, or Mystikal. We played a lot of video games and cut class to play ball in the gym. I was the life of the party wherever we went.

I had yet another mask when I was in the streets of New Orleans or Kenner. I had to be more defensive, more on guard, and protect the people I loved. Basketball kept me away from the drugs, gangs, and guns that were all around me for the most part, but I still had to be aware of what areas were safe and which ones weren't. If we heard gunshots, we ran. When the police came, we ran. If a fight broke out, we watched first and ran once the police or adults were called.

And I had to be those three different people. My survival and ability to fit in greatly depended on my ability to wear "the mask."

Many times my peers and I were asked to try things that put our manhood on the line, like sleeping with certain girls or sneaking out of school just to say we did it, and wearing the mask I wore at home or at church or even playing basketball would have meant getting hurt or possibly risking my life. There was no way to pick one of these identities and just be — I had to be all of them at different times.

I clearly remember a moment where, if I'd come across the wrong person, I doubt I'd be here to write this. One of my friends was dating a girl who invited him over to have sex. The girl had a sister who needed someone to hang out with while they fooled around; when my friend asked me to be that person, I yielded to the peer pressure. I couldn't share this with my mom, so I lied about where I was going. All I had to do was be back before my siblings got home from school, which gave me about ninety minutes. Of course, the girls' father came home unexpectedly. Apparently, a neighbor called to let him know that two guys were seen going into his house.

Their dad chased me around the couch until I was finally able to escape into the backyard, jump the fence, and run down the street. By the time I was halfway there, I realized my friend wasn't behind me. When I went back, I found him walking out the front door with his shirt half-off, as if we weren't at risk of getting hurt or worse by these girls' father.

On our way home that afternoon, things got even worse. As we crossed the street at a four-way light, a cop pulled up next to us. He let his window down, and I could see the gun on his lap. I urinated down my leg a little, scared out of my mind. As a young Black male, I knew that interactions with cops could go bad, fast, even though all we were doing was walking home like any other kids. My mind immediately went back to a previous interaction with an officer, that led to me being thrown against a neighbor's home and forcefully frisked because I "fit a description."

This time the cop asked us where we were coming from and where we were going. We told him that we were heading home from a friend's house, and I told him I played basketball to let him know that I was a good kid who spent more time on the court than in situations where I could get into trouble. Thankfully, he let us go. With another cop, we might not have been so lucky. When I got home, I vowed to never go anywhere alone with this friend again.

I'm so appreciative of the praying parents and grandparents that I have in my family. I'm sure there were many occasions where I could have ended up in a very different place but for the grace of God.

Being a teenager meant social pressure from my peers and questions that came with every situation. Should I do what these guys want so I can remain a part of the group? Do I do something dangerous to remain cool and not be the butt of every joke? Or do I walk away and be the guy that everyone else expects me to be — the talented basketball player who could get a scholarship and possibly go pro?

It was a constant choice to belong or not belong. It would have been easy if the choice I made on Monday carried through till Friday, but it wasn't. My peers and I had to make the choice everyday, multiple times a day, and there wasn't a class to teach us how to handle it.

Parents might believe they have a good handle on what their kids are doing or experiencing. But the truth is, there are more opportunities for kids to be away from their parents than with them. Kids aren't going to tell you everything, regardless of how great you think your relationship is. Some of that has to do with societal pressures, particularly with men and boys, that you're not supposed to tell your parents everything. A man is "supposed to" figure things out on his own — supposed to test limits to see how far he can go without going over the edge.

At the end of the day, struggles like this are just a part of childhood. It's being a teenager. It's figuring out manhood. It's a journey from being boys to being men.

Throughout this journey, I had my best friend, Micah Hagans, by my side. Up until we met, I didn't have anyone around my age to hang out with since my siblings are much younger.

He lived up the road from me in Kenner. Our neighborhood was a mix of cultures, colors, and views, and we were two of the many kids around. While some of those other kids played sports like us, some ended up going down a bad path, into drugs and violence. Others became successful. It was a neighborhood filled with families just trying to make it.

Anyone who met Micah could tell that basketball was his life. He wore basketball clothes literally all the time and carried a ball around everywhere he went. You could usually find him cracking jokes and entertaining, which made everyone want to hang out with him. Girls considered him cute too. This made him confident, nearly to the point of cockiness. That was either a good thing or annoying, depending on how you felt about him any given day. According to his family, he's been like this since birth.

I always knew where we stood as friends, even if the situation might not paint that picture. I remember one day I fell asleep when we were resting at a coach's house before practice in Baton Rouge, only to be awakened by Micah putting a lizard on my face. To him, it was just a joke, but I was so mad and embarrassed that I couldn't stand it. He never apologized for that, but then again, the unspoken rule was that you never said sorry to your friends — apologies weren't cool. You just said "my bad," and either fought about it or moved on. I wasn't a fighter, so I moved on a lot.

Basketball was the cornerstone of our friendship. We started playing together in our neighborhood, where he and all the other kids would play in front of our house whenever it was sunny. He was much better than me — he had been playing organized basketball for longer and his dad was his coach. He studied the game and knew how and why plays would work. His ball-handling was elite for his age and he was a natural point guard. His love for the game and commitment to getting better were contagious.

The competitive spirit between Micah and me was intense, but positive, especially when I look back at how much we both grew our games during that time. We challenged each other constantly — to run harder, to practice more, to do better. We pushed each other out of our comfort zones. Everything was a motivation for us to be better than we were yesterday.

When we played together, things just gelled. Our team at Roosevelt Middle School was undefeated and won the middle school championship. Back then, we didn't know how good we were for our age. We were so tight that when we started getting recruited for high school teams, we said we'd only go as a package deal, even though I was one grade ahead of him. We didn't want to go into a program that was already winning — we wanted to make our own mark together. Eventually, we decided to play at Bonnabel High School. He also advocated for me to join the AAU team he played on, the Louisiana Dream Team, which took us to an even higher level.

By being so focused on basketball and getting better at it, we held each other accountable and stayed out of trouble off the court too. Our lives were totally school, basketball, and video games — no parties, no hanging out. We were at the gym, or we were at home. If one of us got into trouble, it was like both of us did — sometimes literally, since Micah was around a lot. I didn't want to let him down, and he didn't want to let me down. We stayed out of trouble so we could keep practicing and hanging out together.

There was a clear split in our neighborhood between the kids who were into sports (or another extracurricular activity) and kids who weren't. The kids who had sports in their life didn't have as much idle time; the kids who didn't have a way to stay busy ended up going to jail, getting into drugs and gangs, or worse. Between basketball and our families, who stayed on top of us so we did the right thing, we were set up to achieve our dreams.

Our happiness was based on success, not going out and having fun. Michael Jordan, our biggest inspiration, talked about "the cost of success" in the documentary series *The Last Dance,* and I get it. There are probably normal experiences that we missed out on between practices and school, but we couldn't do both. Ultimately, basketball and working towards our goals for the future won out. I don't regret it.

I'm grateful for Micah's friendship, especially since we met at such a rough time in both of our lives. His parents were going through a divorce and I was still adjusting to the new normal after we left Michael. We spent nearly every single day together, sometimes even nights after practice. I had a tough time letting people in because of the traumatic experiences life had thrown my way, but he was there for me regardless. Around him, I could be myself. He took my mind off of what was going on at home with his (usually) funny antics. We had the same struggles, too — with basketball, friendships, and growing up in a culture that constantly pressured you to do the wrong thing; we could talk the problems through. We shared everything.

Basketball kept us both out of trouble for the most part. Sometimes we'd skip classes to play ball in the gym, especially on game days, or we'd run up the phone bill talking to girls — little wrongs that didn't have big, long-term consequences

But still, basketball didn't free us from all of our social problems. The basketball environment was filled with hypermasculinity on steroids, just like the streets. Fights would break out over bad calls since there were no referees, people bullied, and everyone hated to lose. Everything — from how you dressed, to the way you moved, to the way you played — was a reflection of your manhood. The guys who scored a lot of points or could defend the toughest match up gained their status and identity there. If you got dunked on, you were over.

That hypermasculinity even came out between the two of us. Since Micah's dad was a coach, he'd let us into the gym so that we could get in some extra practice. We played one-on-one and almost came to blows. After that, his father said we couldn't play one-on-one unless he was there to make sure we wouldn't end up fighting.

At one point my desire to get better grew. I learned how to be tough and to persevere. Before I'd played for fun, and now I had to play to win. That meant I needed to practice, a lot. Micah and I held each other to this high standard.

Soon, basketball became more than just something I loved to do. Basketball presented an opportunity for me to make it out of New Orleans and get an education. I also had dreams of being an NBA player, but I didn't really think it was possible. It was just a dream, like so many others who dream of playing some type of professional sport.

My mom made a lot of sacrifices for me to play basketball, especially because playing on an AAU team meant I had to travel a lot, and it required an unusual commitment from the coach or the parents of the other players, since my mom couldn't come to get me most times. Many of my coaches stepped up, sometimes feeding me or even letting me stay the night at their houses. I'm forever grateful for all of those sacrifices and for everyone who made me feel like my NBA dreams were possible. The first moment I felt like those dreams were in reach was when I met coach Dannton Jackson.

I was a freshman at Bonnabel High School, and he'd come to watch a player on the opposing team at our home game. I played really well, though I don't remember if we won or lost, and Coach Jackson went up to my dad, who had come up to see me play, and my mom after the game. He told them he wanted to give me an opportunity to play on his team, the New Orleans Jazz Adidas team.

This invitation literally changed my life. Though the AAU team I was on with Micah travelled locally and played in tournaments, this team got a lot more exposure. They also got invitations to many elite camps and tournaments that allowed me to be seen by every college coach in the country. I immediately started getting letters from Division I coaches after our first tournament.

My mom and dad also gifted me a car when I learned to drive in my sophomore year, so I wouldn't have to rely on getting rides from coaches or friends. This made it easier for me to get even more practice time in. She saw that I was committed to keeping my grades up and staying out of trouble, and I saw that she was more emotionally available, so our relationship was in a good place. She trusted me with a car. Of course there were rules, but the car really did provide an extra layer of security. I'm sure it allowed her a few extra nights' rest knowing that anywhere I had to go, Micah was with me — he practically lived with us at that point. Even though Micah wasn't invited to play on the team, he was invited to come work out with us at Xavier University. With a car, we could go up to the Xavier campus every day after practice or after school to go and work out with Coach Jackson.

Working out with Coach was a whole level up from what I'd been used to with my team at Bonnabel. I remember the very first workout I had with him. I didn't score a single basket in our pickup game, and the conditioning after wasn't any easier. I fell out on the floor and even threw up. It was ugly. I was cramping in places not typical for me, and I didn't feel like I had anything else left in the tank.

"You've got two options," Coach said to me. "You can get up and keep going, or you can get out of my gym."

Say what? I thought. Out loud, I said, "I'm a freshman in high school and these kids are in college. Give me a break."

Then he said something that defined my life for years to come: "No, you've got to determine whether or not you really want this. Do you want to be good, or do you want to be average? If you want to be average, you don't need to do this. You can be average by yourself. If you want to be great, you need to get up and push through."

I was being forced to make a choice in the moment. I didn't have time to think about it. I couldn't phone a friend. I couldn't call home and get some advice from Mom.

And I decided to get up and keep going.

What I learned in that moment was that my mind may tell me that I have nothing left, but my capacity is greater. This would really begin to define a new work ethic for me, building off the foundation my parents and grandparents laid for me. Now I knew I could push myself further than what my mind thought was my limit.

From then on, I committed to being there every single day, which meant that I had to be a master at managing my calendar and my day. I got up in the morning before school and went to the gym to do jump shots and work on some ball handling. I went back during lunch to shoot free throws. After school, we had our team practice and after that, Micah and I would go to Xavier University and do whatever they were doing there, like conditioning or drills to focus on certain skills.

There were many days when I was tired, when I was hurting, when I was cramping, when I was sore. But I kept going back.

I found yet another mask to wear when I was on campus. The guys on the team already saw me as a little brother, so I had to mature to be taken seriously. I was quiet and observant instead of the life of the party I was when I was with teammates my own age. Plus, Xavier had some of the most beautiful Black women I'd ever seen (it's no coincidence that my now-wife started her college education there). They gave me a little more motivation.

That first summer I spent with Coach, I never scored a point during workouts. The guys were just too good — too fast and too strong. The only time I did manage to score was when it was one on zero. Micah and I thought we'd been working hard before, but being around older guys taught us that we had a long way to go. We went from the top, straight to the bottom. There were so many new drills and challenges we couldn't keep up with — I felt like I didn't belong.

But Micah and I were determined to make ourselves belong. On every drive back from Xavier, we'd talk through what happened and how we could improve next time. We lost, but we weren't defeated. It was easier to go through this with someone to lean on; together we could stay motivated.

When I went back to my high school practices and games, it was easy. I was so much further advanced than my peers. I became confident that no one else my age or close to my age could beat me, because I worked so much harder than they did.

My motto became, "If you don't work as hard as I do, you don't deserve to beat me."

I told myself this every time I stepped onto the court in my high school games. *They don't deserve to beat you,* I thought. *You're going to shut them down. They don't deserve to be on the same floor as you. They haven't sweat as much as you, they haven't been up at five o'clock in the morning running in the sand, they haven't run levees. They haven't been to the edge of their own capacity and pushed through.*

Even though this mental shift increased my confidence, it was the opposite of the teachings that I received most of my life from a religious standpoint. You're not supposed to be cocky as a Christian. You're supposed to be humble, caring and loving. And yet in basketball, I could be a little more selfish and take a little more risk. I could be more aggressive. I battled between trying to be the nice guy and wanting to be a good player. I wanted to be great. I wanted to dominate.

The more I went out there with those college kids, the better I became in every area of my game. I went from averaging ten points a game to averaging nineteen at Bonnabel. And it was really easy. That's the best way for me to put it — the other players just didn't have a chance. For the first time I started feeling like I was good.

When I went into sophomore year, things were different.

The New Orleans Jazz Adidas team went to the All-American invitation-only Adidas ABCD Camp. I think I was only invited because I was part of this team — we all went. Everyone there was ranked in the country, but I didn't even know they were ranking kids. People talked about the other players, names like LeBron James, Dwight Howard and Glen "Big Baby" Davis. Everybody seemed to know who they were except me, because my life was literally church, school, basketball, video games, and family That's it.

I went out there and I was terrible. I mean, absolutely terrible. I looked out of place. I felt out of place. I remember going to Coach Jackson and saying, "I don't think I belong here."

But Coach said, "If you didn't belong here, I wouldn't have brought you. Now you see that there's another level, so now you've got to work harder. You could be better than these guys if you're willing to put in work."

I'd played for a number of coaches up until that point, but no one believed in me and challenged me the way that Dannton Jackson did. He wasn't only willing to say these things, he was also willing to work with me to get there. Up until that point, the advice I'd get from people in the community was mostly vague, surface-level stuff like, "You got to work on a hook shot. You get your hook shot like Magic, you know? You got to shoot the ball up high like Larry Bird."

But with Coach Jackson it was, "You should work on your ball handling — let me show you how, " or comments like, "You can't be missing shots that you're supposed to make because then you won't have the confidence of your teammates. They're not going to just keep giving you the ball. So when you get opportunities, you got to make them count."

I was just like a sponge, taking it all in. I put in the work and I went back and averaged twenty-two points a game in my junior year. And it was easy, because now I could hold my own against the college kids I'd played against at Xavier. Now I could defend and score in different ways.

I also had advice from my Dad. Now that Michael was out of the way, our relationship could really grow; we could relate on so many levels when it came to academics and basketball, since he also excelled at both when he was my age.

Because of how well we related, Dad was one of my best sounding boards. After my games, we'd talk through things I could improve on or things I did well. When he saw that I had a unique confidence on the court at an early age, he encouraged me to stay coachable and to be the hardest working player on the team. As my skills continued to grow, he saw that I might be able to play college level ball, just like he did. Our conversations started to shift into what college recruiters looked for — a positive attitude and leadership skills for example. This advice was invaluable to me and strengthened my focus.

I valued our relationship so much that at one point, I contemplated leaving my mother and going to live with my dad in Mississippi. I could have gone to the same high school that he went to, so I would be able to glean from his experiences and his teachings and truly become the best basketball player that I could be.

As much as I really wanted to do that and feel like it would have been a great environment for me to be in, I couldn't shake my sense of responsibility to be the man of the house for my mom, brother and my sister. I could not abandon them. I just could not leave my mom. Regardless of how things started out, we were in a great place then. I took the responsibility to take care of my family very seriously. My mom and I were a team, and I wanted to be there to talk things through with my siblings if they needed me. I knew what it was like to be without someone who got what you were going through and I knew how much having others to talk to can make a difference. I also had a great relationship with Coach Jackson, so I eventually decided to stay.

I'm glad I did, because I continued to grow as a player. My team went to the ABCD Camp again that next year and I played in the All-Star Game, walking away as the number nine small forward in the entire country.

I couldn't believe it. I was so proud. To have set a goal, put in the work, committed to it and accomplished that goal felt phenomenal. Making the All-Star team was one of the highlights of my entire life. I couldn't wait to get home to tell everyone. When I got back, we started to have different conversations around basketball.

Before the all-star experience, I was getting the letters from local colleges — the same offers that most people who scored higher than ten points a game in high school got. Now, every single day I was getting letters and phone calls from colleges and universities across the country. Each time my mom went to check the mail, there were letters from coaches sharing how they loved my work ethic and how they would love to offer me a scholarship to come to their school. I could have gone anywhere I wanted to.

At that time I was also getting free gear from people associated with the AAU league. Clothes would just show up at the house, unsolicited. This was important to us because again, my mom was working two jobs and going to school at the same time. We didn't have the money for me to be wearing the latest and greatest Adidas outfits and shoes.

I was able to share some with Micah — we were in this together just as before. Being a year behind me in school, Micah got to learn what to expect when he got recruited. It was surreal for us; we knew we worked hard, but seeing that two kids from Kenner could get to this level built my confidence.

I received shoes that I could practice in and shoes I could wear to games. I loved wearing sweats, so they sent me sweats. I wore them to church, to school — everywhere. Whatever I received, I wore, because it was all brand new stuff, just for me.

Everyone should be treated like a really good athlete at least once in their life.

But don't get me wrong — I still had to work hard. I still had to be focused and keep my grades up. But now I didn't have to worry about my manhood being challenged. Because now, everyone saw my talent. Everyone saw me dunking on people while wearing all this cool stuff. People wanted to be friends with me. Girls who didn't give me a chance before wanted to date me. Now I could relax. I wasn't getting into fights, not that anyone wanted to fight me. I wasn't the butt of any jokes. Things had changed.

But the reason it changed was because I now represented a part of manhood that most guys want, and that is to be a great athlete. I was tough, strong and fast. I had crowds going crazy every time I scored. The newspaper wrote about me and college coaches took me out of class just to talk about basketball. I went on trips around the country to visit these schools.

My brother and sister were my biggest cheerleaders. In Senimon's case, she literally was — she got to be a high school cheerleader when she was in middle school because I played. She'd practice her cheers and raps in front of Mom, and all of them would make posters and noisemakers together. Being recognized as my younger siblings gave them a certain status at school too.

My mom made it to every home game during my junior and senior years, too. My grandparents were right there as well, as was my dad. Dad was traveling from Mississippi, but he made it to every home game during my junior and senior years. My family made sure that I remained humble and that I didn't let this success and attention get to my head. They helped me stay true to my core — the nice guy, the respectful guy, the guy that cared about people, the guy who gave of himself to others.

For the first time, I felt like I'd found my identity. I could finally start to take off "the mask." Now I could be the church guy, the athlete and the family man, all at the same time. As a great athlete, your masculinity is challenged in a different way. Everyone can see you dominate on the court or on the field, so you only have to prove yourself to your teammates or other guys with status. It's like levels. Once you pass the general public level, the challenges come from guys on the same level as you and above.

People stopped asking me to do certain things to prove I was a man. It just stopped. It was like the entire city was on board with helping me remain good so that I could realize this dream of getting to the NBA.

It was truly a phenomenal time in my life, easily one of the best.

After a wonderful high school experience, I decided to go to Vanderbilt University. It's the best academic school in the SEC and one of the most prestigious universities in the country. It would allow me the opportunity to be different, to not be compared to all the other great players that had played in a particular school's history. I could truly make a name for myself, an opportunity that most other schools could not offer.

It was going to be a huge change. In Kenner and at Bonnabel, I was treated differently because of my abilities, but I was still part of the community. I was a star, but not a superstar.

Going to Vanderbilt meant stepping into superstar territory.

CHAPTER 5

Living the College Dream

Vanderbilt ticked a lot of boxes for me. It's not only the best academic school in the Southeastern Conference, but it's one of the most prestigious academic institutions in the country. It has a good basketball history with some great teams and players like Perry Wallace, the first African American basketball player in the SEC.

Vanderbilt was also home to the late David Williams, the first African-American man to be an athletic director in the SEC and who was well-respected for his leadership, emphasis on diversity and inclusion, and commitment to the student athlete. There was also Candice Lee, the first Black female athletic director at Vanderbilt and in the SEC. They both became my mentors in my college career, and were a major reason why I ultimately chose Vandy.

I had become accustomed to a strong support system, which the staff at Vanderbilt could provide as well, and despite their solid program, there was still a lot of room for me to make a name for myself. There wasn't a nationally-recognized basketball program or professional team in Nashville. I could truly stand out and become a big name in college basketball.

The minute I stepped on campus, it was clear that other people already thought I'd become that big name. People had heard of my basketball talent and wanted to make sure they got a chance to know me and vice versa. I signed autographs and took pictures with other students all the time. Folks would yell, "We love you, Shan Foster!" out the window of their cars.

All of this was before I even touched the court.

It was incredible, yet all so different and new to me. I'd had a lot of conversations about academics and playing basketball, but before I arrived, no one told me about what to expect on a social level. I definitely enjoyed a lot of it — I'm a big people person, so I loved getting out there and meeting fans. I never turned down requests for an autograph or a picture, and always tried to make myself available for speaking engagements at schools or community events. Since the season hadn't started, I didn't feel the pressure to perform.

Just as he did in my high school years, my dad helped me navigate that success the right way, and helped me understand how to handle certain situations based on his own experience in college basketball, and that of other high-level players he knew. He reminded me about the kind of person I was deep down, first and foremost. Both he and my mom helped me stay grounded, which I'm grateful for — to them I was always just Shan, their son, not Shan the celebrity. Attention and the drive for exposure can drive people away from who they really are, especially if no one's around them to set them straight.

My teammates enjoyed the same sort of attention for the most part, especially when the season started. I also had teammates who didn't enjoy the spotlight, yet all of them put the team above everything else. It didn't matter whether one player got more attention than another — everyone pushed everyone else to be their best.

Vanderbilt wasn't only a huge adjustment in regard to the attention I got — it tested me in almost every way, right from the start. The academics were one of the biggest challenges. That's the thing about going to Vanderbilt as an athlete — you're in an environment where you're asked to not only compete on the basketball court, but also in the classroom. Before the very first test I took, I spent all night studying, read every chapter and reviewed all my notes until I felt confident I could do my absolute best. I scored my jersey number — 32.

Things weren't off to a strong start in my social life either. While it was fun hanging out and doing things that a lot of college students do, I wasn't interested in drinking. I didn't even drink until I turned twenty-one; I had no interest in being the guy who was passed out on the pavement, so I usually sipped Gatorade or water all night.

But with women, things weren't smooth either.

The dating culture on campus was different from high school. There wasn't much judgment around sleeping with a lot of people — it was just something everyone did. Women were the topic of conversation most days, like who was with who, what they did. The conversations weren't always disrespectful — we often talked about women with sincere admiration, yet crossing certain boundaries just became a part of my life. Through it all, I remembered the respect I'd seen women treated with early on in my life. But now, from every other direction — my peers, pop culture — I was getting a different message.

At first, it didn't seem like there were many consequences for talking like this. It almost felt like it was expected of me as a man and as a star athlete. Eventually the consequences of my actions came crashing down on me.

A girl I was all in on, who I'll call Elaine, ticked off a lot of boxes for me — she was smart, from the south, and played music. I thought that she was the one I was going to be with and that was that. We had talked some and seemed to enjoy each other's company. We even kissed. I thought everything was going in the right direction.

But I was caught up in the kind of masculinity that had become familiar. Guys boasted about the girls they dated or the girls they were trying to date all the time, and I did the same. In all honesty, I knew the guys would be impressed by me getting her because almost all of us agreed that she was the most attractive girl on campus. This is another unwritten standard passed down from other men. Attracting beautiful women is seen as a reflection on you and can raise your status with your friends.

One night, I talked to some other guys on campus about Elaine. I just didn't read the room well — I was seventeen at that time and made a bad decision. Unknowingly, I was talking to a guy who knew her well. Also unbeknownst to me, Elaine had a boyfriend already, though the relationship wasn't going well.

Her friend went back to her and told her that I was only interested in having sex with her and wasn't the guy I said I was.

The next time I saw her, Elaine politely told me that she was no longer interested in dating me and that we could just be friends. Of course, I tried to backtrack because ultimately, what her friend had told her wasn't a hundred percent true. Did I want to have sex with her? Of course — this was what people were doing in college. But I wanted more than that. I wanted a relationship with her.

The situation hurt, especially since I was the one who had taken the opportunity to be with this girl away from myself. I should never have had that kind of conversation with anybody, let alone other guys. I paid the price for it.

Things were even more difficult when it came to being in more intimate relationships. I'd gone from the kid who was trying to not be bullied to the kid that everyone liked and wanted to be around. I'm sure many people starting college experience this. They may have been seen one way in high school, and then have to deal with brand new issues in a new environment without their parents, and likely for the first time. There were girls who wanted to talk to me because of basketball back in high school, but this took it to a whole new level.

I always tell people that temptation isn't temptation unless you actually have access to it, and suddenly, I had access to it. It's different when women *want* you, when they send you messages and show up at your dorm room. That was true temptation.

Temptation was particularly strong because I was in a relationship with a young lady on and off for four years, who I'll call Cee. She was from Ohio, but had roots in New Orleans like I did.

We met in our dorm on one of the very first days at Vanderbilt and quickly became friends. Eventually we started dating. She was pretty, but that wasn't the only thing that I was attracted to. I was drawn to her fun-loving personality and to her intelligence (she was studying neuroscience, which is difficult anywhere but especially at a school like Vandy). And we were both extroverted — if there was a party, she wanted to be there and usually she really wanted to be there with me.

My relationship with Cee was another place in my life where I did what I knew how to do — compartmentalize. It was clear that we were in an exclusive relationship, and I wanted to be in one and make her happy. Honestly, I think part of me has always been the relationship type.

At the same time, I was tempted to explore other people even though I knew that doing both truthfully wouldn't be accepted. But I tried, sliding on different masks in different situations.

I was confused with myself, and the messages from the outside weren't helping. College is seen as a place to explore, but no one tells you how to explore in a healthy way. You have only outside signals from the media, church, or your peers, or your experiences from the past, which might give you conflicting messages.

For instance, my uncle would always ask, "Do you have a girlfriend?" When I finally said yes, he asked, "How many?" At the same time, I saw my grandparents in a loving, respectful marriage. Looking at my peers, I saw that hooking up wasn't a big deal — it was just how it was. No wonder young people can feel like they're being pulled in different directions. We do what we see until we see differently.

So, I tried to be faithful, but it wouldn't last. I would be a great boyfriend when I needed to be, then I would be interested in others when those opportunities arose.

There were a lot of elements that contributed to the situations I found myself in. I've always felt more comfortable around women than men. Part of that was due to growing up in a household and a church that were mostly women, but another was my genuine interest in getting to know people. Most conversations with guys didn't have the substance I was looking for. We mostly talked about sports, girls, rap music, cars, and other superficial things. With women, we would talk about our life experiences, faith, dreams, family, feelings, and everything in between. With women, the range of conversations was limitless.

I fell in love with the process of getting to know someone different — what they liked, what they didn't like, how they became the person they were — and connecting through our life experiences. It was never entirely about sex for me, though I did have some friends with benefits.

It was hard to be just friends with a girl without people constantly asking, "Is that your girlfriend?" or "Are you gay?" So dating became the way I got to know women and become friends eventually. I've gotten to know women through meaningful friendships, but the intimacy is so much greater in dating. I was infatuated by the depth of the conversations.

Sometimes I'd find myself "catching feelings" for the girl in the process, which made things even worse. I would break it off since I didn't want to leave Cee for someone I met on the side.

At college, sex was much more of a motivating factor in these relationships. Sometimes the sex continued past the dating phase and complicated things dramatically, especially since I had no intentions of being monogamous in those casual relationships. After my first sexual encounter with a girl at fourteen, I wasn't prepared for the natural craving for those feelings after. Those feelings and college sex culture only led to more people getting hurt.

Another big part of my difficulty in maintaining a monogamous relationship was that I took Cee for granted, which I only realized years later. I didn't realize how much she willingly chose to endure, daily. While the other women I dated could be there when it was convenient, my girlfriend had to deal with all the things that weren't — like my bad breath in the morning and my desire to be left alone after bad games.

You'll always mistreat those you take for granted. When you don't appreciate the little things, and if you have an eye that's always checking out what you think you're missing out on, you'll miss the one person who truly cares and would do anything for you. This is especially true in the dating world today, where there are endless options to swipe through.

I remember thinking that if someone was "the right one" it would make me more committed, but that isn't true. Being committed is a personal decision that has more to do with you than it has to do with your partner. There's nothing a partner can do to make the other personal faithful — each person has to choose accountability for themselves.

While I know there are no excuses for toxic behavior — and I do think cheating falls into that category — there is way more cultural messaging that encourages playing the field rather than making a commitment, a sharp contrast from the strong, loving example my grandparents and other people in my church community set as I was growing up. I got an understanding of how my peers saw dating first hand. I actually had one girl tell me, "Why are you in a relationship? You're not supposed to be with any one person. You're supposed to be for the people."

This completely blew my mind. I had no idea that dating around was something women expected of me too.

On top of that, we shy away from talking about sex and relationships in general. Commercials objectify women's bodies and use them to get the attention of men. Pornography is more normal than sexual education in schools. Places of worship typically shame people for bringing up the subject before marriage. Most parents are uncomfortable talking about these things with their children. Some of them might cover the big picture things, like using protection, but when it comes to the talking about complexities of relationships, like being transparent about your emotional needs, or the importance of vulnerability with your partner, they freak out.

Sex education in school (if anything beyond abstinence only education is offered) teaches you the basics of pregnancy and protection, but there's no class in managing the urge to have sex. Everyone has to figure that out on their own, and many times that leads to young people forming attitudes about sex and relationships that cause harm in real life. Adolescents are exposed to more media, and by extension, more sexual content in media than ever. Most of that time, the messages are all about the perceived positives of sex or about relationships that are shaped solely by physical attraction. Combined with the still-developing brains of adolescents, these messages can cause serious damage that may impact them far into their lives.[7]

When I was trying to figure it out, I made a lot of mistakes and left some women broken-hearted. I did things I can never take back, though I've certainly learned from them. Not everyone does.

One of those lessons came in my senior year. I was with Cee, but I'd met another woman who I also wanted to be with. She was a model finishing law school in LA. I liked her and couldn't pass up the opportunity to be with a woman all my teammates would be jealous of. It was almost like the fantasy that so many people, both men and women, aspire to in one way or another.

So I dated them both, except the model knew my truth. I could be honest with her without any judgment because she knew I was in a relationship but didn't care. I talked to her about the frustrations in my own relationship, the high cost of living in LA, her brother who played basketball, and more. She was also in a relationship with a guy who played in the NFL, who was sometimes emotionally and physically abusive to her. We spent a lot of time talking about ways she could leave him and why she tolerated the abuse. I didn't know much about the elements of domestic violence at the time, but I knew it was wrong. I shared my own experiences with domestic violence with her, hoping she'd feel less alone.

My ability to compartmentalize caused me to draw a distinction between how he treated her and the unfaithfulness I was putting my girlfriend through. I would say to myself, "Well, at least I'm not doing *that*."

Eventually, she left the NFL player and wanted to be exclusively with me. My heart was still with my girlfriend at Vandy, so when I tried to break it off, she was upset. She found Cee on instant messenger and told her everything.

I still don't know why Cee decided to stay with me, but she did. I know she loved me with her whole heart. I hate the heartbreak I caused her. It wasn't right or fair to her.

College was the training ground for these kinds of experiences. I was grasping at straws and going through different struggles that had the potential to change who I was at my core.

And I wasn't the only one. College students experience pressure from all sides, especially now with social media being as big as it is. Some take their experiences and learn from them or find help, but others might slide into habits that affect their relationships for years to come. Because so many issues that young people really need help with are seen as taboo, they can end up feeling isolated, like no one else understands. But other people can. Other people held me up. Just as it was when I was growing up, I met a few key people who helped me find my way and stay true to myself. They let me make mistakes, but also let me correct them.

My academic career was one of the major places where other people lifted me up, since it was a struggle at first. I remember calling home to tell Momma about it when all of the academics and athletics got to be too much. "I don't think I can do this. I think I want to come home. I'm not even playing. This is just hard," I said.

In her usual way she joked, "Well, if you want to come here, I think Sam's Club or McDonald's is hiring."

I didn't like the sound of that.

But then she added, "I thought your goals were different. I thought you wanted to be an NBA player and accomplish some great things. I think you can figure it out." She knew more than anyone — she'd raised three kids and gone to school at the same time. She challenged me to figure it out, and said that if she could figure it out, I could too.

I decided to find some other students who were doing well in the classroom so I could learn from them. I learned how they studied and how to read the syllabus to make sure I focused in on the specific things professors were looking for. I went to every study group I could. I even fell asleep on the floor of my friend's dorm room after a long day of workouts or games because we still needed to study just a little bit more.

I made mistakes along the way, of course. I often had to learn the hard way. I had to go before the Honor Council for plagiarism as a freshman. Time management wasn't on my side and I was drowning between all the workouts, required reading, group projects, and papers. I had someone else work on my paper and they didn't cite references. Thankfully, I was given a second chance, though if I had any further violations, I would get expelled. I was scared straight, needless to say.

Fortunately, we also had tutors and the coaches were committed to helping me out with the workload. With their support, my friends, and some recommitment to my academics, I made the adjustment and soon started to thrive in the classroom.

Another person who saw potential in me and provided stability and guidance in all areas of life was Bishop Joseph Walker III, the pastor of Mount Zion Baptist Church and now the presiding bishop of Full Gospel Baptist Church Fellowship.

Since I'd been a part of church my whole life, I wanted to find a place to go in and worship when I moved to Nashville. I attended a few services at Mount Zion Baptist Church and eventually not only joined, but reached out to the church's offices to speak with the pastor. It had more than 30,000 members then, and it's even bigger now.

I honestly didn't think the pastor would call me back, but when he did, I told him that I was now being thrust into a life that was throwing new things at me everyday. I didn't know if life was going to be great or if it was going to completely suck. I didn't know what kind of challenges and temptations were going to come my way. I knew that regardless, I needed to be covered and I needed a church family to hold me accountable. He offered his help.

We eventually met in person and continued to meet regularly throughout my years at Vandy. He usually picked me up, along with my friends Joel and Olu, who were students at Meharry Medical College, and we'd go to PF Chang's or The Cheesecake Factory to talk. He was always transparent about his own life struggles, which encouraged us to be the same, building trust between us all. He gave us book suggestions and homework that challenged us in ways that were real and applicable, and that helped us find direction in our finances, relationships, and lives in general. It was the kind of environment that I'd been missing, and the meetings gave me much-needed perspective.

Bishop Walker not only counseled me through our conversations, but through his actions he taught me things that have helped me in every area of my life. He sits on numerous charitable boards in Nashville and continues to be recognized for his commitment to the community. Although his church is massive, he's still incredibly approachable and handles the ups and downs of being a public figure with grace and integrity. He made me realize that you're never too big to not be friendly.

He also showed me how important respect is to leadership. Leadership is about serving, not about power or being in charge. He always emphasized that to me and made sure that I lived that out. It's been an important key for me — everywhere from the basketball court to my work in the movement to end violence against women.

My relationship with him was critical to the boundaries that were set for me during my college years. I certainly got into trouble, like my experience with the honor council. I definitely did things that I regret and that I wish I'd handled differently. I'm not perfect by any stretch of the imagination. I'm grateful for grace.

But when I look at the spectrum of behaviors and actions that were possible, there were limits that I set for myself. A large part of that was due to my faith, which was grounded by my mentors and family. It also made me realize that when someone mentors you, you almost become their representative. When a mentor decides to bring you into their life, you have a responsibility to put your best foot forward. I didn't want to do anything that would be an embarrassment to those I was connected to.

Once I settled into Vanderbilt and found a support system away from home, I learned how to minimize off-court distractions so I could maximize my on-court potential, as my academic advisor and great friend, Cornelius Clark, said. I could focus on the court without thinking about the test that was coming up or a paper I needed to write. I went out less and committed to being in the gym more often. That isn't to say I didn't have fun, but I definitely changed my priorities.

Even though I didn't start out playing much, honing my focus on my education and my game allowed me to take on the huge learning curve that was playing in the SEC. At that level, everyone is good. Everybody averaged thirty points a game in high school; everybody could run, jump, handle the ball, and shoot. It's those who perfected the skills who went on to be great.

These people I met off the court — and many others I haven't mentioned here — gave me the support I needed to focus on what I'd come to Vanderbilt to do — get a world-class education and hopefully reach my goal of playing with the NBA. They were willing to see the good in me and tell me the truth so I could be the best version of myself.

This is something adults minimize in their conversations with youth. Young people need a support system outside of the people who are connected to their parents. Young people need more than one place to go for help and to be transparent. I could show up with mud on me and they would clean me up without making me feel like dirt.

I wasn't very different from other college students. Going from being a child to being more of an adult is a difficult time for everyone. But what made a big difference for me was finding people who I could talk to freely and get support from. Now, more than ever, people are disconnected from communities and their families. Social media is helpful in opening up a channel for you to reach others, but it doesn't replace building a solid support network.

Talking and having open conversations can truly save lives. If I hadn't been able to reach out to my mom, or to my friends, or to Bishop Walker, I could have spiraled off into a life that I wasn't meant to lead. We can't let young people flounder in such a transformative period, even if the conversations are uncomfortable.

Of course, I can't discount how my coaches, teammates, and fans pushed me to reach my fullest potential either. Everyone on campus expected a lot from me, and they were the ones who helped me take my game — and my life — to one of its peaks.

All my life's experiences were coming into focus. Little did I know that the biggest challenge would be upholding greatness.

CHAPTER 6

Becoming Legendary

The pressure of starting my basketball career at Vandy didn't hit me until the season started. My teammates had high expectations of me, but nothing more than what they expected from anyone else. We were going to push everyone to be their absolute best no matter what.

I put most of the pressure on myself because I didn't want to underachieve in comparison to my own standards. I needed to prove that I belonged in the SEC and deserved to be considered as one of the best players in the conference. I had a lot of work to do.

In some ways, it felt like the time I'd gone from playing on a regional AAU team to Coach Dannton Jackson's AAU team. Our conditioning program was leaving me sore and gasping for air while it seemed like more seasoned players breezed through it. It felt like I was on a steep learning curve all by myself. There was so much I didn't do instinctively that my other guard teammates did, like passing the ball to post and handling the ball against pressure.

That's the thing about playing in the SEC, and college basketball in general. *Everyone* is good. It's those who perfected their game that went on to be great. At that point, I was nowhere near great.

I didn't play much at the start of the season, maybe two minutes per game, usually when we were up or down by twenty. It was a big change from high school where I started all four years, averaged over twenty points a game, and was the #9 small forward in the entire country.

It was a hard adjustment, especially when I thought about what the other schools had offered me — starting positions, a certain amount of playing time, resources, and exposure. But I didn't choose Vanderbilt lightly, so I knew that I had to fight to meet my own expectations. I had an advocate on the coaching staff who would constantly reassure me that I was good enough and smart enough to produce results, but I just didn't believe it yet.

Coach Stallings told me honestly, "I'm not going to give you a position over a senior. You have to prove you're better than he is." I knew I needed to go back to my work ethic from high school to get there.

I'd gotten too comfortable with my new normal, staying out as late as I wanted, knowing I had the freedom to do what I wanted, when I wanted. I'd lost sight of my goals: getting an education and playing basketball. At that point I wasn't playing the way I needed to or working as hard as I needed to.

I pulled my goals back into focus, starting with managing my calendar. It was much more complicated than it was in high school, where most of my schoolwork was done during class. In college, this wasn't possible. I planned every minute of my day, from when I woke up to when I went to bed. My day was packed, working out, lifting weights, or practicing three times a day. The rest of that time was devoted to studying, hanging out, and sleeping, just to wake up and do it all again the next day.

The first time I scored in the double digits, it was like a weight lifted off my shoulders. I knew I could do this. I even learned something I hadn't known about myself — I could perform well under pressure. By the time the season was over, I had some twenty-five-point games, having led the team in scoring for some of those, and made the SEC all-freshman team.

Even though I saw strides in my own game, we weren't very good as a team my freshman year; we hadn't gelled. I really liked Vanderbilt — it got me out of Louisiana (which has both good and difficult memories for me), but it was still close enough for my family to support me and come to games. I grew to love Nashville and built relationships that I still have today.

The support from the community and fans lessened the pressure to perform. After bad games fans would tell me, "Don't worry. Just keep working hard and your time will come." But still, I hadn't come to lose. After my sophomore season, I contemplated transferring to a different school where I could have a better career. I spoke with my dad, my mom, and my pastor about what transferring might look like. To this day, I very seldom make big decisions without consulting the wisdom of elders. They suggested that I go talk with Coach Stallings about it, which I did, with two of my other teammates, Alex Gordon and DeMarre Carroll.

The three of us felt that the negative energy surrounding the program hurt our ability to win in such a competitive conference. The dedication and work ethic just weren't there. Sometimes we'd lose a game and players would be thinking about going to frat houses to party. Alex, DeMarre, and I played with emotion and lost with emotion. We'd shed tears in the locker room and people got cussed out — players against players, coaches against coaches, coaches against players. Working hard without a payoff and then seeing our teammates not care wore on us.

Coach set the mood for the program daily too, a mood that made a lot of us dread coming to practice. There was a whole laundry list of little things that had to be perfect just to have a normal practice. If we weren't on the court warming up fifteen minutes before practice, we were considered late and had to run sprints. If an academic advisor reported any issues, we had to run sprints. If anyone had an attitude or missed some sort of appointment or didn't memorize the quote of the day — sprints. That kind of mood made people enter the gym with a defeated mentality and took away the joy of the game. We couldn't win games with practices like that.

Although he was old school and somewhat stuck in his ways, Coach realized that we were willing to do everything it took to turn things around, and that change couldn't happen without his complete buy-in. He saw we were all serious about transferring, and knew our concerns were genuine. We eventually came to a common ground.

If Coach was more positive and created an enjoyable practice environment, the team would have more fun and thus work harder. That way, Coach would also enjoy his job more so all of us could work to accomplish our goals.

The biggest change we made was in our energy approaching practice. Alex would run around getting our teammates excited and I would get our coaches excited. We'd say, "We're 'bout to have some fun today! Let's go!" and talked trash during stretching and warm-ups to build competitive energy. We worked hard, but had fun doing it. We held our team to high standards on the court and off.

Ultimately, Demarre chose to transfer to the University of Missouri, where his uncle was the head coach. There he could get the offensive opportunities he wanted, that he couldn't at Vanderbilt. He still plays in the NBA today. Alex, however, decided to stay.

As you can guess, I decided to stay too, so I could help bring these ideas to life and continue what I'd already started at Vanderbilt. The friendships and relationships I built would become a network for me after college if I didn't make it into the NBA. Having a degree from Vanderbilt is second to none, too, so I wasn't going to give that up. Also, I had already started learning important lessons that would shape me into who I am today, such as what it means to lead a team.

Going into my sophomore year, I was featured on some magazine covers and had a higher profile, which put some new expectations and responsibilities on my shoulders. I was also voted captain of the team, so my conversations with coaches now centered around what my role would be from a leadership standpoint. I was the captain of my team in high school, but doing this on a college level was a whole new story.

Thankfully, in addition to seeing leaders like Bishop Walker and Coach Jackson throughout my life, I'd gotten to know my teammate Jason Holwerda, who Coach Stallings had me room with the summer before my freshman year. We became friends, even though we were technically competing against each other; we both played the same position, but he was a starter and a senior. I had to fight to take his spot.

Jason taught me a lot on the court, but his leadership off the court had the biggest impact on me. He was an incredible leader. He wasn't afraid to call guys out if they were slacking off in practice or in classes, and they listened. He held others accountable for their social lives too. He'd say, "I don't care if you go out, as long as you're ready to bust your ass the next day." And he practiced what he preached. When everyone else went out, he usually stayed in with his girlfriend or hung out on campus.

Following his example was a good start, but my time as captain really taught me how to be a servant leader, which I've taken to my leadership off the court. A servant leader leads by example, and never asks anything of others that they haven't done or are currently doing. They hold themselves to a very high standard and most importantly, they are always looking to make the people around them better.

As a leader, it was my job to make sure that everyone's strengths were firing on all cylinders and that we were staying away from our weaknesses. We needed to challenge each other to be better on a regular basis, to hold each other accountable both on and off the court. I wanted to be a steadying force, lifting other guys up and being there when they needed me to be, whether for just talking about life or for working on our game. It was like high school again in some ways — I could be the person that others came to when they needed a sounding board.

We were stronger together, and as a leader I had to be the glue. When it came to basketball, I would call people on the phone on my way to the gym to get them to come join, or make sure that our workouts, conditioning, and nutrition were all on point.

Off the court, I made sure that we went out as a team. At least every week or two, depending on what was going on, we just went out and bonded. Whether it was choosing our class schedules, eating lunch, doing extra workouts, or just relaxing — we were always together. The more we hung out, the more we built that trust. The more we understood each other, the more we were able to give each other the benefit of the doubt.

Trust and togetherness go hand in hand when you're talking about winning basketball games and knowing how to win in general. You know someone will always be there to back you up if you aren't having a great night, both on and off the court.

We also spent more time doing work in the community together — without them, we wouldn't have the support that we needed to become an even better team; we wanted to give back whenever we could. One of the most memorable fundraisers we were a part of was helping a fellow Vanderbilt student, Kelly Finan, build a playground for the disabled children at the Susan Gray School, on campus. I helped with the planning, and my teammates signed autographs for fans.

The shift our team went through showed on the court slowly at first; after my sophomore season, we did better, but we still hadn't achieved our goal of making the NCAA tournament.

Going into my junior year, though, is when things really started to come together. We struggled a little bit for our first four games, probably ending up with a record of one in three or two and two, losing to teams we shouldn't have. But the ultimate measure of a man is not what he does in times of comfort, but in times of hardship — it's the same for a team. Great teams have the ability to bounce back and pivot.

We knew we all had to be on the same page and we had to sit down and figure this out together. Derrick Byars, Dan Cage, and I were the captains, so we called a team meeting to talk it out. Even though we were used to being leaders, we were nervous about how everything was going to go, how the others would respond to our changes in strategy.

We challenged everyone to really think about the team as a whole. What were we doing well, and what could we build upon? How could we dig deeper, give more, and be more selfless and committed? Everyone was allowed to speak freely — the upper classmen felt more comfortable doing so, but everyone was given the chance. Even though the idea of putting all of our difficulties out there was scary at first, it ultimately was the best thing we could have done. This is where the togetherness piece really grew into something that reflected on the court.

Another big change, both for the team and for me personally, was the arrival of our new coach, King Rice. Coach Rice played at the University of North Carolina and was best friends with Rick Fox, who played for the Lakers and the Celtics. King brought to Vandy the wisdom from his own experience and that of his friends.

Coach Rice reminded me of my coach Dannton Jackson — he was the type of coach to get in there with you. He didn't just tell us what to do, he showed up. He was the kind of coach to call us and say, "Hey, I'm on the way to the gym, you coming?"

And when we went with him, he pushed us. He wanted to be in shape so he could really work with us on the court.

Having someone there to push us past our comfort zone was the key. He constantly reminded us that we had enough within us to get it done, and that we were the only ones who could do that for ourselves. He knew that we were capable and that we could put in the work.

Everyone needs someone who's willing to get in there with them, to push them to the best they can be. Coach Rice would sit in the gym with you when you were putting up a thousand shots, encouraging you to not leave until you did. He'd stay in there until your ball handling was tight enough to go to the basket with confidence. He'd even suffer through post-workout ice baths with you. Coach Rice was there for conversations about life and family. He told me to be the man I said I was, and though I didn't always get that right, I've always come back to it. It's the ultimate goal — be the person you say you are, even if that's constantly changing.

Another change in my basketball career was my dynamic with Derrick Byars, a transfer from Virginia. He was a year ahead of me and had started to play a little during my sophomore year, his junior year. Honestly, I was a little wary of him at first. I had no idea what our dynamic on the court would look like. Off the court, we were like brothers, even literally in some people's eyes. Sometimes people would confuse us because of our heights and builds. We just got each other, even though we're pretty different. He's shy and quiet, more observant, while I'm more of an extrovert.

And on the court, we respected each other's games. We worked out together outside of practice and always wanted to be in the gym. But still, I wasn't sure how we would handle working with each other during games. Coach Stallings reassured me that we'd mesh, and talking to my dad confirmed that. Eventually, we did.

Now going into his senior year, he was touted to have a great season. I was too, and we had the beginnings of a great team. Derrick and I were like Batman and Robin all year. Sometimes he would take the lead and sometimes I would. Most games we scored at least forty points combined. Derek became the co-player of the year with Chris Lofton from the University of Tennessee. Derek eventually went on to the NBA.

By the end of the season, the team was running like a well-oiled machine. We'd lost only one home game that season, beat the highest-ranked teams in the country, and set all kinds of records. We even beat top-ranked Florida, who had won the National Championship the year before. We got to play in the Sweet 16 that year. It was amazing to see our entire Nashville and Vanderbilt communities behind us as we played on national TV and traveled around the country.

In the off-season before my senior year, I gave it my all. I wanted to be in the best shape of my entire life. I always pushed myself to do extra. Whatever the goal was, I did at least one more, whether it was running sprints, lifting weights, or shooting drills. I watched more film than I ever have before and spent time with coaches just to absorb as much as I could. I incorporated more recovery too, taking an ice bath almost daily, just so I could be fresh enough to do it all again the next day.

This was my last year. What didn't happen this year was not going to happen.

It was also my last chance to play in the Memorial Gymnasium with my teammates, some of whom I'd been with for four years. It was my last chance to see these fans and interact with this community. This year would build what the next four years would look like, whether I would have the chance to play professionally or enter the workforce. I still had dreams of the NBA, so I pushed as hard as I could.

My senior season couldn't have gone any better. We beat the most ranked teams in the country and finished the year undefeated at home. We were the highest seeded team Vanderbilt had seen in a long time.

I was the number one ranked shooting guard in the entire country for most of the season. I broke records, too — I became Vanderbilt's leader in three-point shooting and their all-time leading scorer, which I still am today.

This amazing year culminated at Senior Night against Mississippi State, the best game I've ever played in my life. It was my opportunity to say thank you to the fans, the university, and the whole city of Nashville for welcoming this young, immature boy from Kenner, Louisiana.

I wanted to thank my family too for going above and beyond in their support for me. Vanderbilt was relatively close to home, but that didn't mean they could pop over to Nashville with ease. They wanted to be there as much as they could, even if it meant driving up, seeing me play, driving back right after to go to work the next day. And if they couldn't physically be there, they'd listen to it on the radio and cheer me on from wherever they were.

My mom, my grandparents, my aunts, my dad, and all my siblings supported not only me, but the entire team. Everyone knew where my family sat, and they managed to get everyone else in the crowd excited. After watching me play for years, they all knew the game inside and out.

Senior night was no different. Every family member was there that night, dressed in their Easter best. Even though I knew they would be proud of me no matter what, I had extremely high expectations for this game. As I finished my pre-game ritual of Gospel music, I prayed that I would have one last great performance to give thanks to my family and to the community that had my back.

The game didn't start off as well as it ended. By the end of the first half, we were down by twelve and I had only scored six points –— no three-pointers. Sitting in the locker room, my teammates optimistic but worried, I closed my eyes and had a moment to reflect.

I was pressing the whole first half, trying to get it done by myself. But that's not what brought us to that point. We were stronger together and always had been. I had to get out of the way and play for my teammates — this game wasn't about me, even if I cared a lot about it.

I became selfless on the court, praying the same prayers from the locker room. At about the nine- minute mark in the second half, I hit my first three-pointer and never looked back. The defense kept trying to deny me the ball, but I just kept shooting from farther and farther back. Nothing they did phased me.

My mind wanted to take the credit, but I kept telling myself that it wasn't all about me. My teammates were getting excited as we caught up, even though time was running out. I hit another three-pointer to send the game into overtime. It was the end of a long season, so guys were succumbing to fatigue and cramps. These were the moments where I found myself the most focused.

Mississippi was up by two with ten seconds left on the clock, and we didn't have time-outs left. Their defense pressed me, but eventually our guard, Alex Gordon, pump-faked and passed me the ball. I shot the ball out over outstretched arms.

It was one of those moments that felt much longer than the handful of seconds it took for the ball to get to the basket. I made the shot and the crowd went nuts. We won by one point. It was indescribable. My teammates hoisted me into the air as the crowd rushed the court. Everything that I'd fought for came down to that moment, and the communities that had helped me through it were all there — my family, my friends, all of Vanderbilt, and all of the fans.

Even though we ended up losing in the first round of the NCAA tournament in a big upset, I'd finished what I'd started at Vanderbilt.

I was named the SEC player of the year and was an All-American. I'm most proud of winning the Lowe's Senior CLASS Award, which is given to the nation's leading senior athlete who displays great class, leadership, academic excellence, and service to the community.

There were still moments in my life where I had to wear the mask, and I knew I was a work in progress when it came to masculinity and adulthood — but the award signified that I wasn't lost.

When I look back at all the negative experiences in my life, it feels like it was a miracle that I didn't end up dead or in jail like others in the community where I grew up. I can attribute that to the Nashville and Vanderbilt community. Every step of the way, I had a net to catch me and put me back on the right course: My grandparents. My church. My parents. All my brothers and sisters. My teammates. Everyone at Vanderbilt and everyone in Nashville who cheered us on.

As I prepared for graduation, I reflected on my college experience. The things that came to mind were moments with fans, like hearing a little girl who couldn't have been more than five telling me I was her favorite player, or talking with a young man in high school who looked up to me because his dad wasn't around.

I also thought about the closeness I felt to my teammates and how without them, I wouldn't have been successful. We not only won on the court, but we were able to help our community with fundraisers and appearances to make a difference in the lives of others. We were all submerged in a greater purpose than ourselves.

These moments have made me realize how important it is to live a meaningful life surrounded by a community that raises everyone up. You can work hard by yourself and reach your goals on your own, but being able to have people who are supportive and excited for you when you succeed, and vice versa, is priceless. Even the biggest wins that you make on your own don't come close to the satisfaction from wins made alongside others.

I had achieved two of my major goals: graduating from Vanderbilt and having a successful college basketball career. The next step was the NBA.

CHAPTER 7

The NBA Dream

Immediately after my senior year basketball season ended, we went to the NCAA tournament and lost in the first round against Siena College, a small school in upstate New York. It was completely unexpected. We were a ranked team, a four seed, but we lost by twenty points.

It was truly devastating, especially after a night like Senior Night, but I needed to focus on my next steps: the workouts before the NBA draft.

Just like when I started in a big AAU league, then again in high school and college, I was put in a position where I had to prove myself and work for perfection, not just greatness. I didn't have to make eighteen out of twenty three-pointers once — I had to do it five times in a row. I had to focus on every aspect of my ball handling game. There wasn't room for any weak spots.

I was familiar with some of the other players, since many of us had been invited to the same camps, tournaments, and workouts since high school. But there were other players from all around the world, guys who were still in high school, and guys from smaller schools I'd never played against.

The pressure was on — less than 1% of those who want to get into the NBA actually achieve it, and I wanted to be one of them. Being drafted would be an accomplishment that I could hold onto for the rest of my life, a symbol that I had made it and did something that most people couldn't do. It would mean that all the time, sacrifices, and resources that my family had given were worth it too.

I started taking weekday or weekend trips to New York and Chicago for pre-draft workouts. There are a number of workouts, and the ones selected for each player depend on where you fall in mock drafts and what people expect of you. I received feedback that I could be anywhere between the seventeenth pick and the last, which is a huge range. There are only two rounds, with thirty picks per round.

Once the pre-draft workouts started, it was a different workout in a different city every day for a month. I ended up working out with at least twenty teams.

I had to be in the best shape of my life — it was physically and psychologically challenging on every level. Sometimes workouts would be strictly conditioning, but other times they would focus on basketball drills, athletic ability, and basketball IQ so players could demonstrate every angle of their game.

While I was athletic and could dunk on people, there were guys there who would practically jump out of the gym and move incredibly fast. I made up for the hard skills I lacked with some of the soft skills I'd learned over the years — grit, determination, and consistency. I could shoot well, defend at a high level, and make all the right plays. I also had leadership skills and had good character on and off the court. I felt like I brought a lot of the table.

Still, I knew I needed to improve my ball handling. It was one of those skills that I'd always had to work on, since I came to organized basketball relatively late. Coach Dannton Jackson was the first person to really help me with it — he knew that even though I was 6'5" when I was in high school, I likely wasn't going to get up to 6'10" or taller. My height meant that I would play best as a guard, and I would need to handle the ball well in addition to shooting well. I got better at it during the draft workouts, but I never truly mastered it.

I often think about those pre-draft workouts and how much I emphasized ball handling instead of honing in on the aspects of the game that I was already good at. The truth of the matter is that everybody has weaknesses. There's no perfect player in the NBA, and the draft is a somewhat imperfect process.

Some GMs take chances on certain players versus others, defying all logic. Sometimes they strike gold and get it right, and sometimes they get it wrong. It's more about getting and mastering the opportunity to impress the right person instead of showing that you improved in areas that critics believed were your weaknesses. That being said, the best players typically do get the opportunity to play professionally, whether it's in the NBA, overseas, or in the NBA G-League.

In some ways, being among the best players was a comfort, despite the steep competition. I was proud to be considered for a team and was honored to meet people who liked the way I played and had respect for me as a person. I'd gotten great feedback in the pre-draft interviews with GMs, coaches, and execs. I was humbled by the fact that they'd gone so well, and thought that if my playing didn't get me over the hump, my soft skills definitely would. But still, there was no way to know until it happened.

The night of the draft was a once-in-a-lifetime experience. Everyone who's into basketball is excited to see where the new stars will end up and what trades will be made each year. But for the players, it can be one of the most stressful nights of their life. You don't know whether your dream will come true, or if it'll be one of the biggest embarrassments of your entire life, played out in front of everyone you know.

Not being drafted wouldn't have taken away from the journey itself for me. I had already learned a lot, become a well-rounded man, and helped many people. But so much would have been different if I'd failed. Because of my accomplishments up until that point, everyone expected me to go pro. It was a huge burden to carry, even though they would have been proud of me regardless. It would have been like the looks I got when we lost in the first round of the tournament my senior year, after an amazing season. I didn't want that feeling in relation to my career as a whole.

I wanted the same life for my family that I saw my white brothers and sisters enjoying as I traveled all over the world, too. Unfortunately, the path towards that kind of life is much harder for me as a Black man, and the NBA provided access to that, which was why I felt so strongly about it. That was why I worked so hard. There's a level of respect and a number of opportunities that come along with being one of the few draft picks.

And every pick is worth millions of dollars, the kind of money that changes the lives of your family, your friends, and yourself. That kind of money means freedom — the freedom to live without wondering if your bills will be paid, to eat without considering the cost, to truly help others instead of just offering Band-Aids.

That kind of money made the pressure to succeed even more intense.

There's so much hypermasculinity built into sports, especially at the professional level. In many ways, you have to embody that masculine energy to get there. You have to be stronger than every other guy out there, and you can't show weakness. The idea of "playing like a girl," even if you are one, is seen as a bad thing. It's impossible not to feel you're less of a man if you fail. To fail would confirm that you weren't as much of a man as those who made it, that you weren't as tough as everyone thought you were.

Even though I was nervous, I wanted to make the night special. The NBA draft is a one-of-a-kind event. Everyone who's into professional basketball goes every year, or watches the event on TV if they can't get one of the few tickets sold to the public. Press, media, general managers, and the potential top twenty picks plus their families are allowed to go to the event itself. That year, it was held in Madison Square Garden in New York City.

I'd done a lot of training in New York, so I decided to have my party at Jay-Z's 40/40 Club with all my friends and family. And if my name was called, it would be helpful to be close to the arena.

I literally sat on the edge of my seat, watching the then-commissioner of the NBA, David Stern, call out draft pick after draft pick, handing each player a hat with the logo of his new team on it. I waited for my name to be called, not knowing when or if it would. In between draft picks, we had some fun just being together, like we did at family events back in Louisiana or Mississippi — cracking jokes, telling stories, and keeping the energy positive. My best friend Micah and family were there, and we were paying for the party ourselves. It was going to be much more lavish than the parties we had back home, so everyone wanted to make it count.

While everyone gave me support as they always did, the process was still nerve-wracking, especially when I heard the names of guys who were projected to be picked later than I was. Name after name was called, and eventually the first of two rounds ended. My hope was starting to slip, and I had to take a minute and go to the bathroom, where I just cried. It felt like after sacrificing so much and putting in the work, my dream would be pulled just out of reach.

My agent called while I was still in there, and got straight to the point, as always. He and I had built up a lot of trust over the years; we always kept it real with each other. "We have a few options," he said. "Players who are drafted into the second round aren't guaranteed contracts, so we can wait to see if you get drafted. Or, you could go undrafted and try to pick a team as a free agent."

I had no idea what to do. "Let me think about it," I said, hanging up. There were so many risks involved with either option, and there was so much riding on making the right choice. I sat there, running through every possible outcome.

Eventually, my dad came in. He must have easily seen the distress on my face, because he gave me a hug before he said anything. I told him what my agent had said on the phone.

"I know how hard this is on you, but I'm proud of you. We all are," my dad said. "We'll figure this out no matter what."

I nodded. He was right — I knew he would be there to guide me in the right direction, no matter what that direction was, just as he had every step of my basketball career.

"Basketball isn't everything, Shan. All that matters is being the best version of yourself that you can be."

I took his words in. He'd told me this over the years, but this time the words hit differently. The best version of myself was a good example to my siblings. I needed to follow through. We'd always talked about this night, about how they wanted this dream for me as much as I wanted it for myself. I wanted to show them that with hard work, even dreams this big were possible for them.

I dried my face and took a deep breath. "I'll go through the second round and see what happens. I've gone too far to stop now."

Even though I was still scared, I put on a brave face and went back out to the party.

Eventually, my name was called — I was drafted by the Dallas Mavericks as the fifty-first pick overall in the second round. Hearing the late commissioner of the NBA, David Stern, call my name as it flashed on the screen over highlights from my career was surreal. I got to talk to Donnie Nelson, the team's GM, and Mark Cuban, the team's owner, too.

The Mavericks had one pick during the entire draft and they chose me.

Tears flowed and everyone was proud and excited. Now there were so many new opportunities and ways to change our lives and those in our community and family for the better. I could give back to my community in an even bigger way — to single-parent households and kids who had a love of basketball just as I did. I could give gifts to my family and friends to show them how much their support meant to me throughout the years. I could do it all.

One of the best parts of that night was sharing it with the people I loved. It was the culmination of all the days and nights that Micah and I had spent practicing and training. It was possible because of all the sacrifices my parents and grandparents had made to make sure I could play. I couldn't have made it without my aunts, siblings, and everyone else supporting me from the stands.

It meant a lot for my siblings to be there in particular. Being drafted by the Mavericks just validated everything we'd been through together. I've always wanted to be a positive role model for them. They saw the hard work and sacrifices everyone made and had been some of my biggest cheerleaders. That moment drove home how working hard, focusing on your education and caring about your character and integrity could pay off.

I had to report to Dallas within the next couple of days, where I immediately started workouts, interviews, and all that comes along with starting your NBA career. When I flew in, people I didn't even know were excited for me and what was to come, stopping me in the airport for pictures or autographs. They welcomed me to the city with open arms.

I never want to take any of those moments lightly. Being approached by fans always reminded me of a class I took in college. My professor, Sharon Shields, brought a homeless man into class to speak to us. He had gone seven years being homeless and people would stop to give him money or a meal, or they'd just pass by. No one ever called him by his name.

It really stuck with me. If I was in a position where people I didn't even know called me by my name, I wanted to let them know how much I appreciated it and how important it was to me. If I was living my dream, the least I could do was pass along positivity whenever I could, even in the smallest ways.

But even as I achieved one of the biggest goals I'd had in my life, I would soon be faced with a set of challenges I never anticipated. "Living the dream" forced me to learn the hardest lessons of my adult life.

CHAPTER 8

A Dream With A
Double-Edged Sword

After the high of being drafted by the Dallas Mavericks, I set-tled into the next chapter of my life. In some ways, it was very similar to starting again on other teams — there was a lot being demanded of me right away.

Seeing the other players really helped set the stage for the importance of work ethic, mastering your craft and truly being great. The first workout I had followed right after NBA Hall of Famer Dirk Nowitzki had his. I watched him for thirty minutes and he literally didn't miss a shot the entire workout. Not one. His attention to detail was admirable, to say the least.

I mostly participated in one-on-one workouts with the coach, and as the NBA Summer League approached, those workouts got even more difficult and specialized. I had trainers for my ball handling and my shooting, and had to quickly learn when, where, and how to expend my energy to keep up. Once the summer league started, I had another layer of challenges. The Mavericks had decided to sign eight free agents, which put them over the number of available roster spots. As a second round draft pick, a contract wasn't guaranteed for me; I would have to fight for my spot.

That was no problem for me — fighting for what I want or felt I deserved was familiar territory. I gave it my absolute all. I scored when I was called upon to score. I defended well. I constantly asked for feedback and was told that if I kept doing what I was doing, everything was going to be fine.

But after Summer League was over, the Mavericks gave me a choice. They felt as though they hadn't seen enough to go ahead and sign me up for the year, so they wanted me to go to training camp where I'd have to fight for a spot again. If I didn't make the roster, I could be released as a free agent, or I could remain under contract with them, play overseas, and come back in the next year to go through the process again when their roster situation might be more in my favor.

I decided to take a chance overseas and ended up playing in Caserta, Italy, a city close to Naples. Initially, there were only three spots for American players, and they were filled by me, Ron Slay, who played at the University of Tennessee, and Guillermo Diaz, who played at the University of Miami. Later on that year, we got a veteran from the Detroit Pistons, Horace Jenkins. They showed me the ropes and helped me get used to life as a professional athlete. Now it was my career and not just something I was really good at, so we talked about what players' careers often looked like and the different paths they could take.

Italy was an incredible place to land. The culture, the people, the food — all of it. Our fans were incredibly supportive. One of the families that was close to the team invited me to their home for dinner, a five-course meal. I'll never forget it. I really appreciated the emphasis on family in Italian culture. Family dinners happened regularly, and you don't get up from the table until everyone else does — you spend the meal talking about life and connecting. It felt like home in some ways, like the time I spent with my family talking about what we learned in church.

But there were a few things that were hard to adjust to. People don't respect stop signs — they just drive. At least I didn't have to adjust to driving a stick shift, like some of my teammates did. My mom was right when she said if you can drive a stick shift, you can drive anything. Some of my teammates had to learn on the spot, which was difficult for them, but pretty funny to me.

In general, the lifestyle of an athlete in Europe is much different than it is in the United States, depending on what country you're in and what team you play for. With this team, we didn't have a team jet and we weren't taking a lot of commercial flights. We usually drove between cities on a bus. Not a sleeper bus — just a Greyhound bus. It wasn't very comfortable, but it was what we had.

There was a lot of wear and tear on our bodies. Depending on where we had to go and how far away it was, we might leave the day of the game, play, then head back late at night. Sometimes we had to practice the next day, and sometimes even had two-a-days during the season, which was new. Our seasons were about forty or forty-five games, which was more than I'd played in college, more than I'd ever done before.

There wasn't a premium on taking care of your body, and back in 2009 rehab equipment and training facilities weren't as advanced as they are now. We had a team doctor, but besides that, we had ice packs and ibuprofen. We had the knowledge we brought with us, and as a rookie I didn't have much experience taking care of my body with that level of activity. The wear on my body there probably took a few years off my career.

During all of these changes, I was still dating Cee and decided to propose. We had been together a while, and she had been flying back and forth to stay with me while I was in Italy. Though it felt like the right thing to do, it wasn't a decision I made for the right reasons. I flew in my mom and my grandmother, and we all went to Rome for dinner. I had the ring, but hadn't told anyone but my mom.

After the fact, my mom and my grandmother asked, "Are you sure this is what you want to do? Are you sure you're ready for this? You both have a lot of change going on." I got very defensive and said that I was doing what I wanted to do. We had been together a long time, I loved her, and she was a wonderful woman. They didn't press the issue.

I also didn't want to make it big and leave the woman I was with. I knew a lot of guys who'd done just that and heard how badly people talked about it. Getting married seemed like the most obvious step.

What I didn't realize was that the entire time we'd been together, it was all about me.

From being at Vanderbilt and becoming a star player with a growing national profile, to now being drafted into the NBA, the spotlight was on me constantly. On top of that, we had moved from Dallas and now we were in a whole new country because of me. Even though she was a student at Vanderbilt studying neuroscience and dreamed of being a doctor, I was the center of attention.

And Cee loved to give me all of her attention and support. She went to every home game she could, cheering for me and waving around signs she'd made, even though she didn't know a lot about basketball. She wanted to be with me all the time, and was open and genuine about her love for me. But I didn't know her deep down. I hadn't taken the time to know her and I didn't know how to build a relationship. Since we'd dated off and on throughout college, I hadn't even had a true long-term relationship before. In all honesty, I was more interested in building my career and keeping it going than I was interested in putting in the work that was necessary to create a strong bond.

While it was a great opportunity to travel and see the world with a new perspective, it was a lot to balance when it comes to identity. You lose some of who you are. She had given up everything to come be with me — her job opportunities, her desire to become a doctor, her friends, and everything that was her "normal". Dealing with issues of identity when you're in your early twenties is difficult enough, but moving around to other countries and leaving so much behind put more strain on our relationship over time.

After we got married, we went back to Dallas and another Summer League started. Even though I had gone abroad for a year in the hopes that the changes in the roster would be more in my favor, they weren't. They brought in someone else who played my position, a guy named Gerald Green, who's still playing in the NBA. Since they signed him as a veteran, they were obligated to play him first.

That meant Cee and I were going back overseas, this time to Antalya, Turkey. Our condo was literally a block from the beach on the Mediterranean Sea. It was an incredible view, but it was also much less Americanized than Caserta. Back in Italy, there was an American military base nearby, so we could eat like we did back in the US and have other reminders from home. But in Turkey, we had to figure it out ourselves. It was just us, and circumstances forced us to spend a lot of time together. We had a condo that was one street away from the Mediterranean Sea, so we often went to the beach just to hang out, though it was rocky, unlike the sandy beaches we were used to. We also tried a few different restaurants, but found the language barrier there was stronger than in other places.

I hung out with Alex Gordon, my friend and teammate from college, too. We'd play video games and sit around and talk. There wasn't a whole lot to do, considering we were in another country, and we didn't know anyone but each other and the women we were with.

The wear and tear on my body caught up to me and I ended up getting hurt in the pre-season. Like in Italy, there weren't a lot of resources to take care of yourself besides ice and ibuprofen, so I was out for the entire season. I tried to come back a few times, but I ended up making it worse.

Spending this much time with Cee was a struggle, as much as we tried. Back in college, we were together almost all the time I wasn't in class or at practice. She always wanted to spend time with me, and I enjoyed the attention and feeling of being wanted, so it was a pleasure instead of a burden. We went to clubs with friends and just hung around, enjoying college life. There was always something going on with the team, so I'd invite her along.

But now it felt different. Being together as much as we were only brought problems up to the surface. The dynamic we had in college where I took care of most things didn't work now that we were married. I was the sole provider and felt that she should have been responsible for everything else in return. I did my best to be nice about it, but I'm sure she'd say it was more of a dictatorship than a partnership in that regard.

She would often say that I was expecting her to be something that she was not, or she felt like I was trying to change her when I intended to articulate my wishes. I didn't want to change her — I just had a different expectation for what marriage was. This was not it.

The biggest problem was me. I didn't know how to build what I saw in my grandparents' relationship in the first six years of my life. I thought it was something you either had or didn't have. Even though there were adults in my life who were in good marriages, talking about relationships in intimate detail to learn how they worked wasn't the norm.

My injury wasn't getting any better, so we decided to move back to Nashville where I could get treated by doctors I knew could help me. Unfortunately, this only put more of a strain on our marriage. I came to realize that we knew very little about each other. I remember doing an exercise in couples counseling where you predict how you think your spouse will respond to various questions; most of our answers were wrong. I think I responded based on the way I *wanted* her to answer and not how she actually would. It was a huge eye-opener.

I also realized that she was no longer committed to being a doctor like we talked about when we were in college, which was a shock that added yet another layer of strain between us. In reality, I shouldn't have been surprised. We hadn't been settled in one place long enough for her to get her career off the ground. If we were going to move to either Dallas or overseas again, she wouldn't get to start anything long-term.

But all I saw was that she didn't want to be a doctor anymore because I was playing professionally. I didn't see the drive or determination that I'd seen in her when we were at Vanderbilt. She was just blogging about her life (and this was before blogging was big). I felt like she willingly didn't want to work and had given up on her dreams. She started her master's degree while we were in Turkey, so she was capable, but she just didn't want to be the power couple we envisioned and were striving to be. After she gave up her program, another passion never replaced it. I'd pictured something different when I thought of married life. I was sold on us being a power couple, living our dreams. But I didn't know how to create that kind of life.

As we grew farther apart, my career was going through changes too. Once I was fully healed, I was ready for a new start in the summer league. I told myself that this was going to be the year I'd play in the NBA, and I was going to give it my all. But the decision was out of my hands — the Mavericks sent me back overseas.

After I'd done everything they'd asked of me and shown my ability, it still wasn't enough. The Mavericks wouldn't release me from my contract even though other teams were interested in me. I was stuck.

I played in Belgium this time, but I wasn't playing well. I was starting to think that maybe getting back into the NBA wasn't in my path and that God had something else for me, though I had no idea what it was yet. Talking with Sanica on one of my trips home, I was literally in tears over it. She had never seen me that way about anything I was passionate about.

Up until that point, I'd always been great at basketball. I hadn't played this poorly since middle school. I'd worked hard to get to play at such a high level, but my energy was gone from the stress of my marriage — I didn't do the extra workouts that had helped me to be successful over the years. I didn't have a good relationship with my coach at all. He believed in me, but that was part of the problem — I was falling below his expectations, so he was riding me a lot. Every practice and every game seemed to go wrong, and everything felt like my fault.

The fans who had supported me were disappointed too. At one point, they even started chanting, "Foster, go home!" It was a complete 180 from the support I'd received from my family, my friends, and the Vanderbilt community.

I didn't know how to get my superpowers back. I missed shots that I hadn't missed since I was a freshman in college. It was like I was suddenly playing chess with dominoes. It was easily the lowest point in my life — everything I'd ever known about myself was suddenly being called into question. If I could no longer play basketball, then who was I? Not only did I make a living at it, but everyone in my life expected me to be a professional basketball player. It's all we talked about — 100% basketball.

If this didn't work out, I couldn't escape the questions and criticism from others. There were literally articles being written about me regularly, and now the hype of being an NBA Draft pick was wearing off. Up until this point, nothing negative had ever been printed about me in the paper. All positive. But now, there was criticism coming at me constantly.

I felt alone, both literally and mentally. I was all the way on the other side of the world from the support system that had carried me when I had doubts or fears or problems. I could pick up a phone, sure, but it wasn't the same. I knew the distance was incredibly hard on my family too, which pained me. We needed each other, but we were just so far away from each other. They had always been there for me, and now I couldn't return the favor.

On top of that, my marriage was collapsing only ten months in.

My family and friends weren't entirely on board with us getting married in the first place, not because she wasn't a great person, but because we were both going in two different directions in life. The death of my father's mother brought this realization into focus for me.

I'll never forget sitting in the living room in Belgium as my dad told me that my grandmother, Annie Lou Thurman, had been killed by a man who was drunk and driving an 18-wheeler. I went numb from the shock. I couldn't believe it. One minute I was answering what I thought was a normal phone call, and the next, my world had been flipped upside down.

I didn't get to spend as much time with my dad's side of the family as I wanted to growing up, but when I did visit them in Mississippi, I spent a lot of time with my grandmother. She would always call me, check on me, and pray for me. When I graduated from high school, she saved up pennies, nickels, dimes and quarters so that she could give me a hundred dollars for my graduation gift. She made her way up to Nashville for my Senior Night game. She watched my games when they were on TV. Her support meant the world to me, especially since she sacrificed so much. I loved her deeply.

The loss was even harder because I'd spent so much time playing ball and traveling the world during the times I'd normally have spent in Mississippi with her and my dad's side of the family. It had been a long time since I'd last seen her. Losing her this abruptly and being so far away was devastating.

After I received the phone call, Cee came out of the bedroom and asked me if I was okay. When I told her the news, she hugged me and asked me if I needed her. I told her no, even though in all honesty, I didn't want to be alone. I didn't know how to express myself in that moment and didn't know how to articulate what I expected from her, a struggle we'd had even before this. It was the first time I'd ever lost someone that close to me, so I had no idea how I felt. I didn't know what the next couple of minutes or hours were going to look or feel like. She gave me the space I thought I needed.

I'd spent so much time trying to "be a man" about everything that I couldn't ask for what I needed. On top of that, my go-to for solving problems was to pay to fix them. If Cee and I had an argument, I'd buy her something nice to smooth things over. If my brother was getting into trouble at school, I paid for him to go to private school instead.

I couldn't pay to fix this.

I went to the funeral alone, leaving her in Belgium. Again, I didn't know how to express my needs to her. She said that she wasn't good at funerals or grieving, and as most guys do, I told her not to worry about it and that she didn't have to come. In retrospect, I should have told her how much it would have meant to have her with me, but I couldn't. I'd gotten so accustomed to toughing it out alone that I didn't know how to share the burden with another person. I realized there was a lot I didn't know about myself; in this relationship I wasn't making any progress to find out who I was.

When I returned from the funeral, I told Cee I wanted a divorce — my mind was made up and we weren't going backwards. She was devastated. We had tried counseling and she wanted to try to work it out. I knew I wasn't who I needed to be and I didn't want to hold her back from being all that she could be either.

I didn't expect it to be as painful as it was to let her go. I really didn't.

We talked when I drove her to the airport for her flight home. I think we were both hoping something would happen on that ride to fix things, but it didn't. Maybe after time we'd be able to see where we stood, but at that point, I was ready to move on. As I helped her unload her things, I realized she was expecting me to change my mind, and when that didn't happen, she looked at me like a hurricane had hit her, and that hurricane was me. She couldn't believe it, and for that matter, I couldn't either. I didn't want the life we were living, but I didn't know much else. I tried to hug her, but she refused. When I got back into the car, I just sat and sobbed. I punched the steering wheel, screamed and yelled. I had never experienced hurt like that before.

But it had to be done. The truth is that even though we weren't meant to be together and the marriage wasn't working out, I loved her and was worried about what would happen to her. I wondered if she'd be able to pick herself back up and find herself again.

In hindsight, I think I blamed her for things that weren't her fault — my career struggles, my grandmother's death, our relationship. So much of that was my fault, but I wasn't mature enough to face myself in the mirror at the time. While our marriage wasn't ideal, I can admit now there weren't really grounds for ending it — I just wasn't "man" enough to fight for it.

I won't necessarily talk about what transpired in the divorce since it's not relevant to the book, but I will say this: divorce often turns people who are genuinely for each other against each other, because the two of you are no longer on the same team. You can't rest assured knowing the other person is going to do things that are in their own best interest; a marital split forces people to take care of themselves.

Some time after we separated, we talked and Cee shared how she felt. She related it to the Bruno Mars song, Grenade — she felt like she'd literally do anything to metaphorically catch a grenade for me, and didn't know why she couldn't get that love in return.

Now, every time I hear that song, I cry on the inside. I never wanted to be that person. I married Cee in the first place because I didn't want to be the guy who made it big, and then left the person who'd been there all along. But that's how it ended up.

Truthfully, it still hurts. I think divorce leaves a scar when the love was real. I'd drifted so far from the path that made me successful; I didn't know how to find my way back, or if I could.

Now I had to let God take control.

CHAPTER 9

Life After Basketball

On top of the problems in my first marriage, my basketball career was going through changes.

The turmoil in my personal life took away from my focus on the court. I had never played so poorly in my life. On the business end, I went through two different agents to try to get released from my contract with the Mavericks in the hopes of testing the waters in the NBA one more time. Finally, I got the chance to do that.

After playing in the summer league with the Mavericks for one more year, they told me they weren't interested in signing me, which meant another year playing in Belgium. Being isolated in another country and feeling overwhelmed with depression from my relationship wasn't putting me on the right path toward healing. I was trying to process everything based on the expectations of what it meant to be a man versus what I truly needed.

Our culture shames men who go to counseling. The only way it's even remotely accepted is if you're going as a couple with a partner. Just going for yourself is admitting that you're not in control, and that's cause for jokes, shaming, and bullying, even for adult men. I dealt with the feelings the best way I knew how: moving on with someone else as soon as possible. I regret this period of my life. I ended up putting my dysfunction onto someone else — or a few different people — as I searched for healing, understanding, purpose, and some sense of normalcy.

A few years ago, I reached out to the women I dated during that period and apologized for not being the man I should have been. They were difficult conversations, ones that I couldn't have had if I hadn't grown as a man. Ironically, one of the people who helped me grow was a woman who I initially talked to as a friend, my now-wife Ariele.

I found her on Facebook as a suggested friend. I saw her picture and wondered how we hadn't crossed paths — she was from New Orleans, the area where I'd grown up. She was wary of me at first — she didn't take athletes seriously since the ones she'd known were seeing a lot of different women and weren't upfront and honest. But that didn't stop our friendship from growing. She was seeing other people at the time too, so a romantic relationship wasn't really on the table. We talked every day, mostly when she was at work. Back then meeting people online was still seen as a little sketchy, so we didn't exchange phone numbers early on. The more we talked, the more the barriers between us fell. She slowly became less guarded and could be as open with me as I was with her.

We built a friendship that became the foundation of our now marriage. It was a relationship built on who we are as individuals, not physical attraction or connection. After six months, we started talking on Skype to validate that we were real people and not catfishes. We only got closer after that. Having someone who I could talk to with no specific motive or intention taught me how to share myself and how to go deeper than the surface. She didn't care about me being a basketball player because she'd never attended one of my games or seen me play. She had never been in the club with me, popping bottles or splurging on a table. I'd never bought her anything, taken her to dinner, or driven her around in my Escalade. She was just intrigued with me as a person at my core, and I was intrigued with her.

Meeting her helped me out of a period of deep depression, of wondering whether I would ever truly be committed to a relationship, or if I was even capable of doing so.

I flew to Houston to meet her for the first time. It was a little scary since we didn't know if our chemistry was going to be the same in person as it was online. But she spotted me — she said I looked about ten feet tall — and things felt right. We went on our first official date, eating sushi and talking until the restaurant closed. I met her sister and her mother, and we got along well.

After that, we flew to New Orleans to meet some of my family. I knew I couldn't handle the idea of being with someone else or seeing her with anyone else, so we took the time to disconnect from other people so that we could truly make our relationship official. I remember her saying, "If we're going to do this, we're going to do it right." My mentor and friend Bishop Joseph Walker had just gotten married and he and his wife, Dr.

Stephanie Walker, had written a book called *Becoming a Couple of Destiny* — I suggested that we read it together to be as intentional about our relationship as possible. Her past relationships hadn't worked out either, so she was on board with the idea.

For the next six months, even as I was overseas and she was in Houston, we read the book together. We talked about it on a drive from Belgium to Paris for her birthday and Valentine's Day, one of the best trips we've ever been on. We created a norm in our relationship to talk and express why we are the way we are, why we think the way we do, and what our expectations are of each other. It was something neither of us had truly done before.

I think dysfunction in relationships has to do with a combination of societal expectations and the lack of education surrounding the intricacies of relationships, especially in an ever-changing world where expectations and lived experiences almost never add up. We see relationships, but no one talks about how our own desires and behaviors work together to create those relationships. The only way to figure out how our partners work is to be open about who we are, what we need, and what we expect so we can understand which compromises work and which ones don't. This level of openness is quite possibly the reason that Ariele and I have stayed together for so long.

Around the time I finished my final season in Belgium and made my relationship with Ariele official, I was traded from the Mavericks to the Utah Jazz. I was excited for another opportunity to fight for a spot in the NBA at training camp.

My excitement was short-lived. After one unofficial workout, before the official ones began, I learned I had high blood pressure and would be released that same day. I was devastated. I couldn't believe it. As many physicals as I'd done in the past, this had never shown up. Now I had been released by the Jazz.

I decided to go play one year in the NBA development league, now called the G-League since it's sponsored by Gatorade, for a great team called the Bakersfield Jam. I decided that this would be my last stop. I needed to put some things into place and ultimately decide what my life after basketball would look like.

Retiring from basketball was one of the toughest decisions I've ever made. It was particularly difficult because basketball gave me hope, a dream, a purpose and an escape. It was a large part of who I was and where I spent my focus. Basketball took me all over the world, often for free. My journey from being a boy to becoming a man was deeply intertwined with basketball, but I would learn very quickly that there was so much outside of basketball that I hadn't known or experienced.

Many men wrap their identity and self-worth into what they do for a living, no matter what that field is. When that identity is threatened, challenged, or ended, men become extremely vulnerable. They might not know what's next or whether they'll be accepted when they do find something new. I believe there are many athletes who go through something similar when they finish their career, especially if it's earlier than they may have dreamed. That process can be even more difficult because athletes must transition from a world where they mattered, to one where they might be insignificant. It's scary to think that people might look at you differently or exclude you because you no longer have the status you once did.

There was so much I was missing when I played overseas. A big factor in my decision to retire was the challenge in being so far from my family. It was hard on all of us. My divorce and my grandmother's death brought the strong need to be near them into focus. As I talked to my siblings, I realized just how much they were going through and how much they wanted me to be there, whether it was for a shoulder to lean on or to attend the big events in their lives. Taking this into account made me realize that my life needed to be closer to them.

When you decide to retire from basketball, and you've not made the hundreds of millions of dollars that some superstars walk away from the game with, you have to get a job at some point. It was hard to accept that I wasn't good enough to have the long NBA career that so many people expected of me. In my case, my life wasn't a complete disaster. — I still had a Vanderbilt degree, a basketball career that brought about many wonderful experiences and accolades, and a support system ready to embrace me and usher me into the next chapter of my life. It just wasn't what my friends and family expected. It was still hard to face.

I didn't have an immediate plan B — I'd put all my energy into basketball. While I have other skills, gifts, and talents, I hadn't been forced to use or improve them. I didn't have real work experience, so unless I started my own business, it would be hard to find a job that paid nearly as well as basketball did. I had to start from the bottom and work my way up, while my Vanderbilt classmates — who'd watched me play and graduated with me — had a six-year head start into their careers.

My success in basketball also meant that I would have to work really hard to build authentic, meaningful peer relationships and earn the respect of my colleagues for my work, not my fame.

CEOs and executives aren't used to folks at the bottom of their organizations getting media attention, being invited to things they aren't invited to, and having meaningful relationships with board members and investors that extend beyond current business.

It was a lot to juggle emotionally, but in some ways, it was exciting.

Being able to find a solid career off the court was the reason I'd chosen Vanderbilt in the first place. It would afford me a lot of options and connect me with people for guidance. One of those people who guided me was the late David Williams. David told me about Archie Griffin, who played football at The Ohio State University and then went on to play for the Cincinnati Bengals. He'd returned to his community and was able to be impactful using the platform he'd built as a player. David said that I could do the same for the community of Nashville.

David was always the one who thought bigger than what I was thinking. I thought I could just come back to Nashville and maybe coach, which I did, or use my basketball skills and knowledge in some other capacity. David challenged me to think about how I could make an impact and how I could do something that would outlive me. Not everyone had the platform to do something in that regard, and I knew I had to take the opportunity.

Ariele, who had joined me in California my last year playing ball professionally, moved with me back to Nashville, where I got involved with the opening of a new charter school, Intrepid College Preparatory School. It started at fifth grade, and every year we added a grade until we had grades five through twelve.

I got involved with Intrepid through another Vanderbilt grad, who was the executive director of the school. When I returned to Nashville to figure out what to do next, I sat down with various people from my network to learn about their careers and see if anything resonated with me. I didn't want to teach but knew that coaching was naturally a possibility. In order to make real money in coaching at the middle-grade or high school level, you also needed to teach.

The executive director remembered me as an atypical athlete with a high level of character who could be a great role model for students; she offered me a position as the school's first Dean of Culture. I taught financial literacy and P.E. and was a grade level chair. It was the perfect chance to gain a lot of needed work experience.

Being on that founding team allowed me to wear a lot of hats and showed me how much I could learn and do. People told me all the time how the skills you learn playing basketball and team sports translate well to the world of work, but up until then, I was only taking their word for it. Now I was able to see how my skills were an asset.

As a grade level chair, I was responsible for leading, advising, and supporting six other teachers, even though I had the least amount of teaching experience. I leaned heavily on everything that helped me on the court — my work ethic, relatability, teamwork, and values. Teachers would come to me with tears in their eyes from the stress and pressure of performing in this fast-paced education environment, and I'd give them my all.

When working with the youth I'd often use my speaking skills from camps and other speaking gigs to connect with them around topics beyond classwork. We'd talk about leadership, social issues, respect, and self advocacy. I'd use quotes from Vandy basketball days like, "you have to act yourself into a new way of thinking" or "in the field of opportunity, it's plowing time" and so many others. Having been mentored throughout my life, it felt like a natural step to help others out too. It was amazing to see how these young fifth graders evolved over the year, mentally, socially, and emotionally

Intrepid was my training ground for what I would be doing next. Teaching financial literacy and running an after school program to teach boys about healthy masculinity gave me an educational structure based on a combination of best practices and my lived experiences to be relevant, relatable, and impactful. This structure even worked when mentoring teachers, leading professional development, or meeting individually with parents. Meeting with the executive director (my supervisor) was like meeting with a coach. I never shied away from talking to her and always spoke with autonomy. She respected that and leaned on me for advice often.

During that same time, Ariele and I got married — the best decision I've made in my life. I now had someone to grow and learn with forever. We vowed that everything we built, we'd build together.

Our wedding was in New Orleans, and she planned everything. The venue was across the street from Canal Boulevard and Bourbon Street, so the ambiance was incredible, filled with candles and lights. I remember Ariele wanted Mardi Gras beads to add to the venue and asked me to run out and find some the morning of. You'd think finding them in the heart of New Orleans would be easy, but it wasn't. Luckily, I ran into my friends Ray, Joanne, and Vinny, who saw me panicking and helped me find those beads.

Our wedding was such a great time. Our families got along well, and during the ceremony we honored our grandmothers, who'd both passed away before we met. As I watched my new wife and my mom dance together, I realized that putting in the work to change and be intentional about your life could lead to better things.

Not long after we were married, Ariele suggested that we make a vision board together, which brought what I really wanted for my future into clearer focus. At the top of the board, I included that I wanted to be a national or international public speaker in seven years. I've always been a speaker at heart, even back in high school at church. Through basketball, I got to speak to the community as well; I truly enjoyed the opportunity to hear the stories of others and how they connected with mine, which ultimately helped me understand how to positively impact people.

Some of the best and most meaningful accolades I've received over the course of my life have been letters from young men and women who were inspired by my words. In the same way I'd wanted to inspire my siblings, my story was creating hope and a strong work ethic in others. Now I could impact even more people, who saw what I'd accomplished and believed they could achieve as well.

After two years at Intrepid, I knew it was time for me to define what was next. I felt like I had given the school and my students my all, so it wasn't hard to move forward. I knew that taking steps towards my own goals would be a good example for my students too, since I always emphasized setting goals and making sacrifices to reach them. I was approached by the Young Women's Christian Association, or the YWCA, to join their new concept of engaging men to end violence against women and girls.

At that time, I hadn't heard a lot about the movement. However, a few months before they sent their offer, I was invited to an event called *A Call to Coaches* by Gail Williams, a great friend of mine and the wife of David Williams. She really took care of me when I first lived in Nashville and still cares for me today. There would be hundreds of coaches and athletes there to participate. One organization, A Call to Men, was there to present to all the coaches. Tony Porter, the CEO, had a conversation with David Williams that changed my life and my outlook on how I could affect the world as a man. They talked about how important it is for men to be role models, particularly in regard to manhood and where many of our ideals and behaviors have come from.

It was so inspiring to listen to. As you've read, wrestling with what it means to be a man and the choices that come along with that struggle have been a recurring theme in my life.

I re-visited the offer from the YWCA. I was interested in the opportunity, but I hadn't heard of the YWCA. However, their mission really hit home for me: their goal is to eliminate racism, empower women, and promote peace, dignity, and freedom for all.

The concept of engaging men to end violence against women and girls connected with me because of what I experienced as a child back in Mississippi and Louisiana. I was reminded of the relationships I saw in college, where the vast majority of young men had no guidance on how to interact with women in a respectful way. It also reminded me of how women were treated in bars, clubs, and in the media, being demeaned and objectified. During that experience I didn't have the perspective necessary to create change in a big way, but now I would.

Everything I had learned showed me that we lived in a world that produced a culture where violence against women and girls — whether it was physical or mental — was inevitable. But, if I learned the intricacies of domestic violence, sexual assault and rape culture, I could engage with men to help them through our common struggle with masculinity and manhood. Ultimately, my life experiences could help tell the story of how men are the missing link to the equation to ultimately end violence against women and girls.

I saw the opportunity offered by the YWCA as similar to what Vanderbilt offered me regarding basketball. I could write my own path and do something that, at least within my sphere of influence, was not being done. I could truly use my life experiences to make the impact that David was confident I could make.

And yes, it's important for us to do the work to provide services and counseling, and to care for individuals who are the victims of domestic violence, — but if we can change the culture, it will go a long way toward interrupting the cycle.

My future and purpose started to click into place. Throughout my life, I'd seen just how much opening up, asking for help, and having positive role models had helped me succeed. I was lucky — I had praying family members, parents who supported my dreams, friends who were willing to tell me what I needed to hear without making me feel like I was lesser. So many others didn't.

I could be part of an organization that tried to give those who weren't as fortunate the role models and support they needed.

I accepted the position at the YWCA as the director of a program that was then called MEND, so I could do just that. Little did I realize that what would become my mission as a man, would create some of my greatest challenges as a Black man.

CHAPTER 10

The Mission Worth Fighting For

When I joined the YWCA, there were only a small handful other men working in our main administrative office and one or two working in the shelter that the organization runs. Out of the men who worked in the office, two were white, and one was from Ethiopia. The only other black man who worked at the organization worked at the shelter in maintenance.

The leadership team was similarly lacking in diversity at that time. The history of the YWCA of Nashville is over a hundred years old and there had never been a president or CEO who was a person of color or a man. I don't say this to be critical — when I joined, YWCA stood for Young Women's Christian Association instead of just YWCA, as it is now, so that was to be expected.

I stood out from the start. I was a very tall, accomplished black man who was coming into a traditionally white female-led organization in a very female-dominated field. The *Tennessean* even wrote a story about how I was engaging in the fight to end violence against women and girls. My fame, especially in the Nashville community, and my gender came up in the interview process. I was asked if it would be a problem for me to go from my basketball career to a role like this and if I was comfortable having a woman as a leader.

To me, my platform was a tremendous value add, and I was very used to women in authority, from my grandmother to my mother to the executive director of the charter school I had just left.

For a while, neither of those things were an issue.

My supervisor and I started with a great relationship. Her primary responsibility was the domestic violence shelter and the program that eventually became AMEND. She took the time to talk with me and made sure that I had a full understanding of the YWCA way of doing things.

We also had deep conversations, which were a prerequisite for this position. Given the emotional nature of what we were doing, you had to be able to be transparent and vulnerable to communicate about things that typically don't come into the workplace.

We talked about racism, classism, sexism, pornography, the objectification of women, and every other issue related to violence against women and girls. Everything seemed fine — we checked in with each other to make sure that both of us were doing okay, so I assumed that they were.

As we talked about these issues, we started shaping the direction for a new initiative program. We started hosting forums and using my gift for public speaking to get people to understand men's engagement in fighting domestic violence. From there, people wanted to get involved to get this message out to the community, which led to opportunities to present to leaders, teachers, and faculty in the school system. We spoke to all-school assemblies, athletic departments, middle schools, high schools and college students.

That led to us outlining an idea that would help organizations engage with men in the discussion of violence against women and girls and challenge the culture that allowed the violence to happen in the first place.

We started with what we called the three C's — clergy, coaches and CEOs — because we felt that if we engaged all three of those audiences, we would be able to reach most men and boys. Getting involved with the clergy engaged the faith community. Many have played some kind of sport in their lives and many coaches were parental figures in their players' lives.

It was important to engage with CEOs because it wasn't enough to just engage with youth. There needed to be continuity between what boys were doing in our program and what they were learning from the community. We needed the corporate community to take a leadership role and reinforce our message.

We also needed to reach men as adults, to talk about preventing sexual harassment in the workplace and beyond. When we talked to corporations, we wanted them to think critically about how to cultivate a culture where women are not just safe, but valued and respected.

The more we did this work, the more people wanted us to come speak to them both locally and eventually, nationally. Though it was exciting that what we had created was starting to pick up steam, the success started to fray on what I'd thought was a solid relationship with my supervisor.

Once we gained national attention, we were invited to different places. I got an email from a national nonprofit organization that was a thought leader in the space of engaging the public in the fight against violence against women. They were putting together a think tank of leaders from around the country to come up with new ways to discuss healthy masculinity with young men. They were going to pay my way and I felt that I should tell my supervisor since I would be going during the normal work week. To my surprise, she said, "Well, they don't know what they're looking for and they typically want an executive to represent the agency when they send these kinds of requests. I need you to ask them if I can go in your place."

I hadn't been in corporate America or at this particular nonprofit, so I didn't understand all the proper etiquette for these situations, but that certainly didn't feel right. As a Black man who had felt racism before, this hit that antenna. I told her I could make this request, but also that it didn't sit well with me. Her response was to talk to the then (now former) CEO of the YWCA about it, who she said agreed with her. Out of obedience, I wrote back to the national organization to tell them what was decided, and they ended up paying for both of us to go.

This was the first time that my supervisor and I really clashed. I started to notice how she tried to exert herself whenever opportunities arose that had some publicity or celebrity attached, even when I was the only one they requested. It was like the first invitation from that national nonprofit over and over again — she always tried to go in my place or asked me to ask the organization to invite her as well.

I didn't join the YWCA to make a name for myself. I'd done that playing basketball. I didn't want to step on anyone's toes — I cared (and still care) about the mission. I feel a desire and a responsibility to all six of my younger siblings to leave the world better than it was for me. I want my younger sisters to live in a world where they're not only safe, but valued and respected. I want them to get paid the same as their male counterparts for the same work. I don't want them to walk down the street getting constantly harassed by men who only want them for sexual pleasure.

I don't want them to worry about being in a relationship with a man who thinks that relationships are all about control, and not respect. Likewise, I don't want my brothers growing up thinking that relationships are like that. I don't want them thinking that women are there to be objectified. I don't want them to be that kinds of man.

That's why I do the work and why my supervisor's actions rubbed me the wrong way.

After I'd been there for two years, the then-CEO of the YW transitioned into another career and our program moved from being under the control of my supervisor to being under control of the new CEO, the person I would report to directly. This change was made in order to help the program move forward — we needed to take what was at the time a well-intended but fledgling program with little focus, and move it to a national movement.

Almost immediately, that was a problem for my former supervisor, making it clear in my view that the program was about control for her. Once she was no longer in charge of me and the program, there was no attempt to collaborate or to work together on any other project. Literally nothing. There were more opportunities, but it seemed like she'd put out a vendetta to minimize our work or make things more difficult than they should have been. She told people internally to avoid working with our program, saying that I was a selfish, bad leader who was hard to get along with. She didn't pass along the few relationships she had cultivated for the program, but instead used them for her own agenda. She took credit for all of the work and even claimed that she founded AMEND Together.

This woman created a rift between AMEND Together and the rest of the YW. People delayed when asked to help with projects, gave little to no effort in collaborations, and scheduled vacations during our biggest events. The tension created a hostile working environment, especially since I continued to treat people with the utmost respect. It wasn't fair, but it was my job, and I refused to let injustice run me away from the work I had devoted my life to.

I'll never forget a meeting I was in with other agency leaders during my first year, where we were having a critical conversation about race and ethnicity. I shared some personal stories about the impact of racism on me and my family. She stood up in that moment and told me with conviction in her eyes that she was an ally and that I could count on her to do her part to change things.

But where was her allyship now? How could she be an ally while trying to tear me down and block opportunities to actually create change?

During a conversation about diversity, this former supervisor said I took our mission too literally. I said that based on our mission, it didn't matter that I was a Black man and getting leadership opportunities, because the first line of our mission statement is "eliminating racism." That means at the end of the day, we should be treated equally here if nowhere else in the world.

The conflict came to a head one day in a strategic planning meeting. In front of the entire executive team, she said that six women had left the organization because of me. She had lied to HR about this too.

Anyone who knows me knows that I care about my reputation. While some leaders could really care less about how others view them, I'm probably someone who cares too much. I want people to see that I care, that I value people, and that I try to the best of my ability to do what's right.

I took this comment as an assassination on my character, to the extent that in that moment, I very seriously contemplated leaving the agency and the work I'd given everything to over that three year period.

Throughout American history, there have been countless Black men who have lost their lives, their freedom, their jobs, and their reputations as a result of being lied on by a white woman.

Throughout my life, I've had to be aware of the things that could happen to a Black man if he was in the wrong place at the wrong time, either with a white woman or otherwise. One incident really stands out in my mind. I was at a frat party my freshman year at Vanderbilt and hit it off with a white girl. We went back to my dorm room and started fooling around. At some point, she froze and said that she wasn't sure if she wanted to continue.

That was enough for me to get out of my bed and tell her to leave. Even though she said she didn't mean that she was done all together, I didn't care. I even put her shoes out in the hallway, as harsh as that sounds. She was a small white woman and I was a tall, athletic Black man. People would see her leave and assume all kinds of things that could have happened, especially since she expressed some hesitation — things that would end up haunting me. Having her stay over was a risk I wasn't willing to take.

It doesn't matter if you aren't doing anything wrong. Once, our AMEND Together high school boys were making Christmas gifts for the women and children in our shelter. While on a break in the common area of the high school, one of the white cheerleaders said to one of our Black students, "If you say anything to me, I'll scream rape."

These are the realities facing Black men and boys. Being in the wrong place at the wrong time. Being perceived as a threat. Just *saying* something to someone. All of these things can destroy a life. I thought I had escaped this, at least within the workplace due to the nature of our work. I was devastated to experience this at the YWCA.

The new CEO called me and said she would get to the bottom of it. Ultimately, an investigation was done and it was found that none of it was true. In order for me to be okay with this and for me to move forward, I said that I needed my former supervisor to issue an apology in the same setting where she'd made those accusations.

I never got that apology and she left two weeks later.

This experience really challenged me to my core. I leaned on my faith and Ariele's support a lot. But I believe that everything God allows, He allows for a reason. If this is the kind of thing that's happening to me now, there must be greatness on the other side of it Thinking back on it, I feel that there were a few things at play in this situation. I think my former supervision started with good intentions, but being an ally is more about what you do when tested than what you do when comfortable. While it takes courage to speak out verbally, attend rallies, and even hire people of color, bias (conscious or unconscious) is proven in moments of discomfort.

The truth is, it's uncomfortable for some white people to be outperformed by people of color. It's uncomfortable for some white people when a person of color is chosen over them, or when they succeed in spite of efforts to slow them down. And most importantly, it's uncomfortable for a white person to feel powerless when it comes to people of color having complete autonomy over their life and career.

And while most would refute those statements, it's been proven in history and currently when situations challenge this. In this particular case at the YW, our problems didn't start until after she was no longer my supervisor and the program was taken from under her leadership. And this was regardless of the rapid success and growth we saw.

Of course, these are things that can be shrugged off as bad behavior and not racially motivated, but that's literally where racism lives — in everyday actions and micro-aggressions that can't be proven as outright racist.

I also learned that given the lack of training, education, and honest discussions around racism, American history has created a culture where white society has certain societal privileges that have been normalized. In many ways, I can relate. I've traveled all over the world and been treated amazingly by most people. I've enjoyed luxuries that most people can only dream of.

My experiences match my expectations, whether it's at a restaurant or with a repair in my home. However, I grew up in circumstances where this wasn't the case at all. So while I get upset when things aren't done according to my expectations, I don't throw a fit or go out of my way to make someone else suffer because I've been inconvenienced, an action that's the result of privilege.

Most of my white brothers and sisters who do racist things don't actually want to be racist. It's just so unconscious that it takes considerable effort to think through how their actions and behaviors might affect people of color. And to make matters worse, they don't have examples of what a life where they take those feelings into consideration looks like, and the topic is so sensitive that it takes a lot of courage to ask for help in this area.

The advice I'd give to white people who aren't sure about how to handle topics of race is to ask.

For people of color, dealing with white people who may not see the racism in their actions: treat them like the person in your family who you aren't particularly close to, but they're family, so you work with them until they learn better. Or said another way, love them until they learn how to love us back. Sometimes love means we give grace and sometimes it means we tell them the truth regardless of how much it might sting. We must stop sugar-coating our experiences and true feelings in the workplace out of fear of retaliation. It takes the same courage that we're asking of white people for us to tell the truth. They'll never see your perspective if you never share it.

And nothing will change if you continue to let things go. Those who are dead set on treating people disrespectfully should suffer the consequences.

I'm very grateful to the leadership of the YW, who did not act in a way I think a lot of other organizations would. There are countless examples of people of color who have been falsely accused and who paid the price, whether it was being put in jail for crimes they didn't do, having their lives ruined, or being killed. Avoiding that fate has become a part of my everyday life. I keep Vanderbilt stickers on my car or wear some piece of Vanderbilt clothing almost all the time, just to signal that I'm educated and not a threat if I end up getting pulled over.

Once I got past looking at the issues that were present even at the YWCA, I started to focus on prevention, and on inviting men to be a part of the conversation and solution — truly inviting them, not telling them what they should do and should have done.

AMEND Together was finally developed and focused. The program under new leadership experienced tremendous growth. We went from a few programs in Nashville to working with twenty-three schools, impacting more than 600 boys on a weekly basis. We're seeing tremendous outcomes in students' academic performance and behaviors. They're understanding the connection between the jokes and the bruises, between the culture and the violence.

We've heard from boys who say it's too uncomfortable to talk about healthy relationships and masculinity at home with their parents. They can't talk about it at church either, where they get abstinence-only education. With sex education being taken out of schools as well, they're left with their peers and pornography to teach them about relationships.

College students tell us that violence and misogyny happen so often that seeing it doesn't bother them the way it should, but no one steps up at all. Many in professional sports say that while locker room talk got flak not too long ago, there's still a lot of conversation that shouldn't happen.

Seeing how well-received AMEND has been has given me hope. As deeply as some of these issues in our society run, we're starting to see that people want something better for themselves and others. Together, we can end the cycle of unhealthy masculinity and violence against women and girls. We just have to push beyond our fear of change to get there.

Conclusion

Being in my fifth year of doing this work at the time of this writing, I've seen a lot of progress through having dialogues about healthy masculinity and how we treat women and girls. I've seen a lot of men getting on board and asking, "What can I do? How can I help? How can I change and do better? How can I be a better father to my sons and daughters?"

People are talking about these issues at the dinner table and at school and work. We're talking about them more than we ever have before, which is a great and wonderful thing. But we also have to recognize the challenges that exist when doing this work.

There's not enough research. There aren't enough support groups. There aren't enough mentors to do the work, though organizations are trying to recruit more and more people, especially people of color.

There are also issues within the same movement. There's the mentality that there's no room for men in a women's movement — the either-or mentality instead of a both/and mentality. We have issues of diversity or lack thereof that remain in every industry, especially in senior-level leadership.

But there's also the mentality that we need men to be a part of the solution if we're ever going to reach one. It's not for lack of effort or expertise that we still have these issues. It's a lack of having the other side of the equation, which in this case is men.

Some feel that men respond differently when they hear this message from a man, in particular a man who they trust or look up to, but others believe that the message should be heard the same regardless of who is delivering it. It's like seeing white people protesting racial injustice. We all know it's necessary, but when it actually happens, it encourages other white people to join in and put actions behind their words. Again, we need a both/and attitude to truly accomplish what we've set out to do.

In our country, so much of what's been built has been built on an either-or mentality where people have to pick a side — politics, churches, schools, social movements. We see all of the work to fight for justice and equality being done but we don't see that work resulting in people no longer needing to do certain jobs because the problem no longer exists.

We're still fighting the fight because so many of us are clinging to the idea of picking one side instead of working together. Despite all the slogans that state that we're "stronger together" or that we'll "solve this together," we still default to working against each other. We know working together is the solution, but it's the hardest thing for us to do.

We need to own this weakness in order to overcome it and get things done. We can move from mitigating problems to preventing them in the first place. Workplaces would be much healthier. We could reap the benefits of diversity and inclusion, where the terms won't just be boxes that people check off to mitigate liability. Prevention is the solution.

These issues are everywhere — no community, ethnicity, race, or religion is exempt. Domestic violence, sexual assault, rape, and sexual harassment don't discriminate.

I didn't think men were going to gravitate toward this message at first. I really didn't. But the more we invited men in to talk about this and the more we diversified we became, the more authentic stories we heard: Men who said, "My father didn't talk to me about this," or "I just didn't know." Men who with tears in their eyes talked for the first time about being the victim of violent crimes themselves, who until then had been too afraid of seeming like less of a man for speaking up. Men who thought about their parenting or leadership styles and knew that they needed to do things differently.

The second key to reaching a world without violence against women is putting in the work. This doesn't just mean posting about it on social media or listening to a speech or two. We need to have those difficult conversations at work or at home, and to be honest when looking at our own behavior, past and present. Like everyone, you've probably made mistakes, but you can grow from them.

This work isn't about me. It's much, much bigger and there are great organizations that are helping to invite men in. But we have to do it together — men, women, boys and girls. We can put in the work to create something better, whether it's ending unhealthy masculinity, racism, discrimination, or domestic violence. We need to be open-minded and willing to change to create healthier relationships and safer communities.

When I look back at my life, all the pain, hardships, disappointments and yes, joy, I know that there was a plan for me. What hurt, didn't hinder my purpose from coming to fruition! I aim to be the best Black man I can be and to lead others in a movement where men put in the work to change a culture that supports violence against women.

I'm excited to help corporations reimagine their culture and its impact on business. It's critical that we move forward with integrity, creating space for authenticity and autonomy. The ROI for diversity and inclusion is tremendous and those who don't get on board will be left behind. We live in a global world. From internet, to travel, to cultural impact, our lives are more connected now than ever before. Because this level of connectedness has not been the case for most who are old enough to work and have climbed corporate ladders, there's so much training and education to be done.

I also look forward to helping parents understand the journey of boys to men, by providing insights into the impactful moments in their sons' lives that must be discussed, validated, and influenced. Auto pilot is great for flights, but detrimental for manhood. We have to reconnect guys' heads with their hearts so that our actions and behaviors will match.

Lastly, I want to continue to help men and boys realize their potential. We've left so much by the wayside by distancing ourselves from the experiences that society has said are feminine. It has cost us relationships, joy, and peace both in the workplace and at home. We must stop making certain choices because that's the way they've always been done, and start doing things because it's the right thing to do.

This movement can't just be either-or. It must be both/and! And we can make that happen.

Discussion and Reflection

Use these questions as jumping-off points for group discussions or personal reflection.

Chapter 1

Wherever you are on your journey, it's important to remember your foundation. **Where did you learn the values you hold true today? Who taught you the principles that have shaped your business, relationships, parenting, or leadership? What experiences from your foundation impact how you treat others, especially those less fortunate than you?**

As you reflect on the pivotal moments of your life, be conscious of the emotions that flare up for you. If you get excited or feel proud in the moment, find someone to share that with. There are those in our circles who didn't get the experience but can glean the lesson from what we share. If it brings up feelings of resentment and open wounds, consider unpacking the origin and seeking to heal that relationship; give yourself grace, and even forgive yourself and others. Whether good or bad, our foundation matters and it influences how we show up in the world today. In order to know who you are, you must revisit who you've been.

Chapter 2

At the time of writing this book, we're in the midst of the COVID-19 pandemic. Tensions are high in all areas of life, from politics to race to family. This time is far from business as usual, but many are still suppressing their emotions the way they did before the world screeched to a halt. While there are various resources and options available for coping with social isolation and stress, they all consist of talking, which is seemingly the hardest thing to do.

Whether it's a parent needing to connect with a child, a spouse longing for intimacy within their relationship, or a manager disconnected from a diverse workforce, people shy away from opening up and telling the truth. The reasons for doing so range from fear of judgment, retaliation, or vulnerability. Regardless of the reason, collectively, we don't talk about the things that we often should, and we are paying the price daily in our families, relationships, and business.

When was the last time you let yourself be vulnerable? When was the last time you spoke your truth and allowed the healing process to begin?

You can't heal what you won't reveal. In many cases, those who have hurt us or disappointed us in some way, may not be aware of the impact it's had on our lives. As a loved one or friend, your relationships reach their potential when all things can be discussed openly. As a leader, it's important to create the space necessary for authenticity and vulnerability. The more we normalize this, the healthier our culture will be. It's usually the hardest thing to do that produces the greatest results.

Chapter 3

Domestic violence not only impacts those directly involved, but also those who witness it. Statistically speaking, boys who witness abuse are more than twice as likely to be abusive. Girls who witness it are more than twice as likely to be victims. The thing that changes this is intervention. As parents, it's important to talk to your children about respect, healthy boundaries, and signs of abuse. These discussions are necessary parts of their cognitive development as early as elementary school. The earlier we teach children what is and what is not a healthy relationship, the better.

In business, it's important to provide resources for those who might need help and raise awareness. The issues that affect people at home will ultimately impact production at work. Those same issues may also affect staff culture due to the team culture many businesses try to embody. When a member of your team is a victim of abuse, it indirectly has an effect. As leaders, we have a responsibility to provide the community resources available, but also ensure the workplace is supportive, safe, and aware.

Have you had conversations about healthy relationships at home, school, or the office? If so, do you feel they impacted the way you approach your relationships today?

<u>Chapter 4</u>

All students need a place to belong. A place where they fit in. A place where they can be confident in their identity. For me, it was basketball. Not only was it something I excelled at, but it gave me friends and accountability. So many students struggle to find what works for them. Those who struggle are more likely to find outlets and coping mechanisms that are unhealthy and cause harm to self or others.

There's a phrase that I think is really important to consider: "It takes a village to raise a child." I'd argue that it also takes a village to produce a good leader. **So, who makes up your village?**

Think of your village as having a personal board of directors. Every person who's a part of your village serves a different purpose. If you're a parent, each child's village should include teachers, administrators, coaches, mentors, spiritual advisors, and parents of their closest friends. We know that external influences are so important; this village allows the parents to have eyes and ears in many places at once. It also creates built-in accountability, which we all need in our lives.

If you're a corporate leader, you too, need a diverse village. Your village should include advisors in the following areas: spiritual, financial, business, health and wellness, family counselor, and personal counselor. It should include people of different genders, race, and sexual orientation. Those who have their own village are more likely to experience balance, happiness, and success in various areas of their life. It goes back to the definition of team — Together, Everyone, Achieves, More.

Chapter 5

Many leaders deal with impostor syndrome. This is deeply rooted in the fear of failure and belief that we're not good enough. Both are wrong. You only fail if you give up, and you're more than enough! In many cases, your struggles, the fact that the path wasn't easy for you, and the resilience you learned along the way is exactly what is needed to achieve your goals. You may have to dig deeper than you have before. You may need to lean on your village more. But if I can do it, you can too.

Do you have a fear of failure, or do you believe that you're not good enough? Can you find three concrete reasons why you're not an impostor, like the goals you've achieved or the obstacles you've overcome to get to where you are now?

Chapter 6

One of the major pieces of advice I received from my dad while I was excelling on the court was to take the time to stop and enjoy the ride. Too often when achieving we get so focused on the next goal, the next obstacle, the next hurdle, that we don't stop to appreciate the moment. Life is short and filled with ups and downs. Some days we're floating on cloud nine, while others it seems we're falling from the same cloud.

Take a moment today to reflect on your success. No matter how big or small, celebrate yourself. Whatever it is, you did it. You won. You achieved. You survived. You made it. It worked out. It's okay to celebrate yourself. It's not arrogant. It doesn't make you conceited. And it doesn't make you self-ish. In fact, it's what makes you human. Yes, you made mistakes and no one is perfect. But don't let it get in the way of progress. There were a few things I'd do differently if given a second chance. I caused some harm to some and was the victim of hurt from others. But aren't you glad that what hurt, didn't hinder? Hold your head high. Celebrate you. Not because you're better than anyone else, but because you're a winner. And all winners deserve to be celebrated!

Chapter 7

Have you ever accomplished something only to realize that the achievement was more about the climb than the final destination? This is more often the case than we reveal. After speaking with leaders across various sectors, I learned that the best teacher is experience. It's your experiences that taught you work ethic, compassion, empathy. It's your failures that taught you grit, determination, and perseverance. It was adversity that taught you humility and charity. And it was favor that taught you grace.

Let's sit with this a while. What lessons did you learn on your climb that prepared you for where you are today? If you were to interview a close friend or colleague, what might they share about your journey from their perspective? Who helped you along the way?

Take out a sheet of paper and make a list of all the people who positively impacted your life. Then I want you to set a goal to call or email them, expressing your gratitude. My family often says, "Give roses while you still can."

So take the time to give your roses to the teacher who believed in you when no one else did. Or the coach who pushed you when you wanted to give up. Or the custodian who left words of encouragement on your desk. Or the family member who always supported you, no matter what. Don't let another day go by without telling those people how much they mean to you. Not only will it brighten their day, you'll be surprised by what it does for you!

Chapter 8

In this chapter I shared some things that it took me years to admit to myself. We all have a tendency to think much higher of ourselves than we ought. I thought I had life figured out. I was living the dream. But I was also torn inside. I experienced the internal dilemma that we all face at some point in our lives. It's the helper who also needs help.; the champ who's experienced failure; the lover, who's experienced hurt. I found myself in this dilemma. And what do you do when what others need from you, you also need yourself?

It's very difficult to do for others, what you haven't gotten right for you. But it's liberating to be vulnerable and ask for what you need from others. But my challenge for you is to be you. The authentic you. The vulnerable you. The messy you. The "don't have all the answers" you. The hurting you. The broken you. The total person, you! It's liberating to live in your truth. Notice, I didn't say that it's easy, but it's worth it.

Is there anything you're giving to others that you also need yourself? What ways can you be vulnerable with someone else today, in a big or small way? What ways can you be your authentic, messy, liberated version of you?

Chapter 9

My mentor David Williams, who passed away almost two years prior to the release of this book, would often say, "I can't always do what I *want* to do, but I can always do what I *can* do, and I will." These words ring true for me everyday, and I challenge you to meditate on these words too.

There will always be things that we just can't do. But as David so eloquently reminds us, there are also things we can do. We should be diligent in seeking those things. We should educate ourselves on issues, processes, and the systems in play so that we are well aware of the realm of possibilities.

And once you've plotted your strategy, it's your responsibility to take action. **What are those areas for you where your passion is great, but you've not found your strategy? What can you do today to create your strategy? And if you do have your strategy, what can you do to make it come to life?**

Don't give up. Don't give in. It's not a lost cause. It may take patience, it may take reconciliation. It took all these things and more for David to bring Perry Wallace and Godfrey Dillard (the first African American athletes to integrate SEC & Vanderbilt Men's Basketball) back to Vanderbilt. And in the seventeen years he served as Vice Chancellor and Athletics Director at Vanderbilt (having integrated SEC Athletic Directors himself), he would tell you that this wasn't possible in the early years. But he did it. And if David could do it, I think he'd say, so can you and I.

Chapter 10

Allyship is only worth what it cost you. It is easy to be my friend when you invite me to dinner and we sit in your place of comfort and convenience, eating on fine china and drinking from crystal glass. However, it means something when you cross the threshold of my wooden framed door. When your feet grace my cold floor. When your back is propped by my dinner room chair and we eat on paper plates and plastic cups. Not because I'm poor, but because I'm different from you, yet the same.

As Maya Angelou said so gracefully, "we are more alike than we are un-alike." When you visit my home you'll see the culture of my ancestors whose blood, sweat and tears gave way to my existence. It means something for you to be here. Not only to eat, but to share, to discuss, to debate, to laugh, but most importantly to just be. Without fear or judgement. Without assumptions, stereotypes or bias.

It's at dinner that one becomes an ally. When one truly sees another for who they are, how they have become, and where they are headed. It's at dinner that we build friendship, care, and empathy. It's at dinner that we build trust.

How can you create more authentic opportunities to break bread with your diverse neighbors? In what ways can you focus on how we're alike versus how we're not alike?

Notes

1. ^ https://munewsarchives.missouri.edu/news-re-leases/2011/0822-males-believe-discussing-problems-is-a-waste-of-time-mu-study-shows/
2. ^ https://scholarworks.sjsu.edu/cgi/viewcon-tent.cgi?referer=https://www.google.com/&http-sredir=1&article=1016&context=themis
3. ^ https://nomore.org/wp-content/uploads/2013/11/VZF_MORE_GfK_Survey_v1.pdf
4. ^ https://www.cdc.gov/violenceprevention/pdf/2015data-brief508.pdf; https://www.cdc.gov/violen-ceprevention/pdf/NISVS_Executive_Summary-a.pdf
5. ^ https://www.ncbi.nlm.nih.gov/pmc/articles/PMC4768593/
6. ^ https://www.unicef.org/media/files/BehindClosed-Doors.pdf
7. ^ https://www.ncbi.nlm.nih.gov/pmc/articles/PMC1070813/

CPSIA information can be obtained
at www.ICGtesting.com
Printed in the USA
BVHW041217281220
PP11678400001B/1

9 780578 825595